Will It Skillet?

Will It Skillet?

53 IRRESISTIBLE AND
UNEXPECTED RECIPES TO
MAKE IN A CAST-IRON
SKILLET

Workman Publishing · New York

Library of Congress Cataloging-in-Publication Data is available.

ISBN 978-0-7611-8743-1

Design by Jean-Marc Troadec
Cover and interior photography by Waterbury Publications, Inc.,
Des Moines, IA
Ken Carlson, Photographer
Charles Worthington, C2W, Food Stylist

Workman books are available at special discounts when purchased
in bulk for premiums and sales promotions as well as for
fund-raising or educational use. Special editions or book excerpts can
also be created to specification. For details, contact the
Special Sales Director at the address below, or send an email
to specialmarkets@workman.com.

Workman Publishing Co., Inc.
225 Varick Street
New York, NY 10014-4381
workman.com

WORKMAN is a registered trademark of Workman Publishing Co., Inc.

Printed in China
First printing March 2017

10 9 8 7 6 5 4 3 2 1

To Bryan

. . . .

Acknowledgments

My thanks to those who bought my first book and made possible this second book. Those who read and supported the succession of blogs I did before that will always have my gratitude; following a story with no discernible middle or foreseeable conclusion isn't for the faint of heart or attention span. (Say what you will about my books, but at least you know when they will end.) Thank you to my editor, Megan Nicolay, for the inspiration and to my agent, Stacey Glick, for the encouragement. I am also very grateful for the efforts of Selina Meere, Jessica Wiener, Lauren Southard, Chloe Puton, Rachael Mt. Pleasant, Beth Levy, Anne Kerman, Jean-Marc Troadec, Barbara Peragine, Doug Wolff, and the rest of the team at Workman Publishing, who have been known to work miracles. To Kerrie Ahern and the small cadre who tested these recipes, thank you for your perseverance and your dedication to saving me from myself. Finally, my mom's feedback has always been valuable—she taught me how to drive, for example, and then continued to provide feedback on my driving for many years afterward—but her comments on the recipes in this book were particularly helpful and made them that much better.

Contents

Introduction

In my first book, I took a look at the waffle iron and elevated it from single-purpose appliance to everyday multitasker. But I heard from a lot of people who didn't have a waffle iron.

And I thought about what is truly indispensable in a kitchen—thought about which single piece of equipment is uniquely versatile and remarkably durable. And I arrived at the cast-iron skillet: that rare cooking implement that is equally at home on the stovetop or in the oven, in a restaurant kitchen or over a campfire.

Let's think about it another way: You are going to a desert island. You can take one piece of cooking equipment. Do you take your saucier? Your slow cooker? A crepe pan, a cake pan, a casserole dish? The tart pan with the fluted edges? No. You take your skillet.

We know it's versatile. But is it even more versatile than we might have thought? This cookbook you hold in your hands answers that question. (At the risk of blowing the big reveal, the answer is yes.)

Of course, this book is more a beginning than an end. As you see what your skillet is capable of, you'll find yourself reaching for it more and more. And your skillet will reward that loyalty by becoming more beautiful and useful. Soon, you may find yourself asking and answering the question "Will it skillet?" Family recipes, ideas floating around the internet, dishes from favorite cookbooks— all of them can be sources of inspiration and all of them just may find a new home in your skillet.

I can't wait to see what you cook up.

1

Before You Begin

Before we dive into the recipes, let's consider a few tips, techniques, and strategies. Maybe you've heard about "seasoning" cast iron and you get the idea it's something you should do. But what is it exactly? You're in luck! I will answer that question. Maybe you're wondering what shape and size your skillet should be. That is here, too.

I also delve into ingredients. Is a cup of flour always the same? Does the size of the eggs you use matter? Butter is butter and yeast is yeast, right? One-word answers: No, yes, no, and no. Now allow me a few more words and I'll lay it all out for you.

Choosing Your Skillet

What's So Special About Cast Iron?

If you're not accustomed to cooking with cast iron, you should be aware of some of its unique properties.

First, let's talk heat. Cast iron is a relatively poor heat conductor compared to, say, aluminum. This means that the heat will travel relatively slowly and perhaps unevenly through a cast-iron skillet, especially as it begins to warm. That said, it stores heat very well, so it will take longer to cool down than other materials.

Next, there's the brute strength of cast iron. It *is* possible to crack it. Leaving it empty on the stovetop over high heat could cause this to happen eventually, but here's the thing: I cannot confirm this from personal experience, because in my decades of using cast iron, this has never happened to me. You're more likely to hurt something (or, I suppose, *someone*—be careful!) with a cast-iron skillet than you are to damage the skillet itself.

Cast iron also holds incredible value. The racks of cookware stores are lined with pots and pans, some of which cost an astonishing amount of money and are far less versatile than cast iron. Is there a place for them? Maybe. If pressed, I will admit that I do own cookware beyond my cast-iron skillet. And yet what do I reach for most consistently? What has held up the best? What was among the least expensive pieces? My cast-iron skillet. (Well, skillets—I have six.)

Skillet Size

The recipes in this book were developed and tested using 10-inch skillets, as measured from outer rim to outer rim. A small variation shouldn't cause a problem, but beyond that the volume of the skillet can change quite a bit. Consider that a skillet 10 inches in diameter with a depth of 2 inches has a volume of about 10 cups, while a 12-inch skillet with the same depth has a volume of about 14 cups. That's a 40 percent increase, which means those 2 inches make a big difference. That difference, in turn, will have a big impact on cooking time and temperature. Some things—stir-fries, crepes, grilled cheese—will be forgiving of the size difference. Other things—cakes, muffins, pizza—will either not fit properly or require a different baking time or temperature—or some combination of both. The bottom line: For best results, stick to a 10-inch skillet at first; the experimentation can follow.

Manufacturers often assign a number to indicate the size of the skillet, but that number should not be confused with the measurement in inches. In many cases, for instance, a No. 8 skillet is about 10 inches across.

Shape and Materials

When it comes to skillet shape, it's useful to have handles on two sides. An empty cast-iron skillet is heavy enough. When it's full of food, having an extra spot to grab on to is handy—particularly when dealing with something hot from the oven.

The skillet should be all cast iron—no wooden handles or plastic knobs or anything else that won't withstand high heat.

The Bottom Line

The recipes in this book were developed for and tested in 10-inch cast-iron skillets. Some recipes are more flexible than others. While using a skillet of another size or material may work in certain cases, it may also affect recipe results.

Seasoning Your Skillet

Here, seasoning doesn't mean salt and pepper. Think seasoned in the sense of "experienced." You're building up resistance in your skillet, keeping it impervious to the foods that pass through, and—ultimately—getting it so slick that an egg won't stick to it. This happens because fats used in the skillet break down and reorganize at very high heat to form an excellent nonstick coating. This process is not instant! (More on this in a bit.)

Many new skillets are sold preseasoned—that is, they come from the manufacturer with the beginnings of a nonstick patina. Buying a skillet preseasoned is a head start, but it's still just a start. Proper use and care of the skillet will build up an even more resilient finish over time. And in the end, there's no substitute for that time.

If you notice your once-trusty skillet has lost its nonstick powers, you may need to reseason the skillet (see Salvaging Cast Iron, page 10).

How to Season

Here's the basic process for seasoning a skillet.

- Warm the skillet slightly over low heat, remove it from the heat, then cover it very lightly with oil or fat (see Choosing a Seasoning Fat, page 6). Use a paper towel to spread a few drops evenly across the skillet, including the handle and the bottom. The coating of oil—about a teaspoon or so in total—should be all but imperceptible. In other words, it probably won't look like there's oil on the skillet, but there is. That's the right amount of oil.

- Put the skillet in an oven preheated to 500°F for an hour until the oil is baked on. (If the temperature is too low, the oil will turn into a sticky coating.) It will probably throw off some smoke. That's part of the plan. Smoking oil is not good for cooking but is just what you're looking for when seasoning the skillet. Once the hour has passed, turn off the oven, and leave the skillet to cool inside.

- Repeat this seasoning process as necessary—perhaps a few times when you first acquire a skillet, and then maybe a handful of times a year thereafter, especially if you notice the coating has uneven, rough, or sticky spots.

Choosing a Seasoning Fat

As to which fat is best for seasoning the skillet, volumes have been written and internet arguments have raged. Bacon fat is fairly traditional, but often not the easiest thing to come by. Flaxseed oil is often recommended; in my experience, it does produce a very nice sheen, but it's hardly the only oil worth using.

Bottom line: Stick to a neutral-flavored oil such as canola, peanut, or corn oil or vegetable shortening. Avoid fats such as olive oil and flavorful nut oils.

Seasoning Shortcuts

One shortcut to a well-seasoned skillet is having someone else do the work for you. If you pick up a used skillet at a thrift store

---

China, Han Dynasty 206 BCE-220 CE

Blast from the Past

The earliest specimen of cast iron is created! A blast furnace converted raw iron ore into molten iron, referred to as "pig iron" in its unfinished state. These pieces were then remelted in a cupola furnace to produce cast iron.

Russia, 1000 CE

Skillet Outlaws

In Eastern Europe, cast-iron skillets are used to make blini, a type of small pancake that is served with cheese or fruit. The cooking process used to be a long and mysterious one: Women left the house to make blini in forests and alongside lakes.

Japan, 17th Century

It's Easy Being Green

The *tetsubin* cast-iron tea kettle was created in Japan in order to make *sencha*, a popular green tea that originated in China. The kettle was said to sweeten the water; it was also elaborately decorated with relief designs, each one unique.

or a yard sale, it may have already built up excellent seasoning from years or decades of use. A good used skillet can be worth its (considerable) weight in gold.

Then there are the not-so-good secondhand skillets, the ones that have been mishandled or unloved. Don't ignore these. A little oil, heat, and care can once again make them productive members of society (see Salvaging Cast Iron, page 10).

Seasoning Pitfalls

Sometimes the coating on the skillet can turn slightly sticky. This is usually because the seasoning oil was applied too thickly, the oven temperature used to season it was too low, or the baking time was too short.

The seasoning process cannot be rushed! Using more oil does not speed the seasoning process or make the skillet more stick-resistant. It just leads to a sticky or uneven surface.

Likewise, being timid with the oven temperature avoids some of the smoke that seasoning can generate, but it also fails to create the magic necessary for a satisfactory finish. A longer baking time can't compensate for a lower temperature and a higher temperature doesn't mean you can shave time off the process.

In any case, if your seasoning is sticky, all is not lost. Scrub off the sticky layer and start over with the seasoning process (see Salvaging Cast Iron, page 10).

Cleaning Your Skillet

Here's the overview: Start with a warm skillet. Use hot water or a loose paste of coarse salt and water to tackle any food left in the skillet. If bits still cling to the skillet, move on to gentle scrubbing with something a little abrasive. Even when your skillet is clean, though, it will still be wet. Dry it over low heat or in an oven on a low setting. Then apply a thin coating of oil to the still-warm skillet. You're done.

Let's take a closer look at the process.

The Netherlands, Late 17th Century	England, 1707	Scotland, 1776
Going Dutch	**Slimming Down**	**Rich in Iron**
The Netherlands had the most advanced cast-iron system in Europe. Dry sand was used to create molds, which produced higher-quality cooking pots. As a result, these thick-walled pots came to be known as "Dutch ovens" (*braadpan* in Dutch).	English Quaker Abraham Darby I patented a new "greensand" casting method that allowed thinner pots to be mass-produced. This strategy extended beyond pots and provided mine owners with iron wheels, steam engine cylinders, and machinery in bulk.	In his book *The Wealth of Nations*, an in-depth analysis of how countries build wealth, economist and philosopher Adam Smith declared that the wealth of Scotland was not in its gold, but in its cast-iron cookware.

Water, Judiciously

It all starts with water. Before you go scrubbing, scratching, scouring, or scraping, start with a rinse to soften anything stuck to the skillet and wash away any loose food. It's true that storing a wet skillet can encourage rust, but that's a far cry from saying that you shouldn't get a skillet wet. Of course you should get the skillet wet! Just make sure that it's well dried afterward (see Put It Away Dry and Coated in Oil, page 9).

Salt, Judiciously

Salt, especially coarse salt, is a fantastic natural abrasive, one that deploys just enough scrubbing power without the risk of going overboard. Mixed with just a tiny bit of water—a few drops will often suffice—it turns into a paste capable of dispatching stubborn food remnants before disintegrating into something that can be rinsed away with the unwanted bits.

Plastic Scrubber

Available in bunches at the dollar store, these lightweight scouring tools are a godsend. They have just enough substance to attack stuck-on bits, and it's impossible to scratch the seasoning of the skillet with the plastic. Rinse them thoroughly to get out the bits of food that will inevitably get caught in the webbing. I've also had good luck running mine through the dishwasher, although nothing priced at 99¢ for five is made to be durable. (For something much more long-lasting, see the next entry.)

Chain Mail Scrubber

In a class by itself for its durability, this is a reusable cleaning implement with some of the same benefits of the plastic scrubber. I resisted picking up one of these for years—*did I need another scrubber in my kitchen?*—but when it arrived, it was love at first scrub. We're talking about an eight-inch square of small metal chain links. (Although I do enjoy the thought of a full-body chain mail suit, it's

America, 1788	Europe, Mid-19th Century	America, 1890s

Everything but the Kitchen Sink

George Washington's mother, Mary Ball Washington, thought her cast iron so valuable that she bequeathed it specially in her will: Half of her "iron kitchen furniture" was left to her grandson, and the other half to her granddaughter.

Call the Exterminator

The most common pan was called a "spider" for its three legs and handle, designed to stand up in coals or hang over a fireplace. The invention of the kitchen stove replaced the open hearth and paved the way for the modern cast-iron skillet.

Iron Pot Hotshot

Griswold Manufacturing was one of the biggest players in American cast iron from 1865 to 1957. Its reach extended beyond manufacturing— the company's founder, Matthew Griswold, was elected to Congress as a Republican twice (1891–1893 and 1895–1897).

probably—no, definitely—overkill for the task at hand.) The rounded metal of the links is just right for getting rid of any stubborn bits of food, while still going relatively easy on the coating of the skillet. One caveat: Scrubbing too hard may ding the skillet's seasoning in places, so start gently and ramp up slowly.

No Soap

Stalwarts warn forcefully against *ever* using soap on cast iron. *It will damage the seasoning! It will ruin the skillet! It's a crime against cast iron! Bad things will happen!* Some of those things are probably true, to a degree. A lot of soap or a very harsh soap will probably do some damage. For me, the bottom line is that, indeed, you should not use soap to clean the skillet. Not because the skies will darken and a chasm will open beneath your feet, but because it's just not necessary. Use the other methods described here and you won't need to use soap. The companion truth to this is that if some soap does happen to meet your cast iron—say, you have a particularly rowdy party and people go off the rails doing the dishes—it'll be just fine. Rinse it off. Dry the skillet. Apply a light coating of oil. Carry on.

Not the Dishwasher

Don't put your cast iron in the dishwasher. It's not top-rack safe. It's not bottom-rack safe. It's a terrible idea.

Put It Away Dry and Coated in Oil

Always put away the skillet dry. To dry the skillet, put it over medium heat on the stovetop, or in a warm oven if it happens to be on, for a few minutes. Once the skillet is dry, remove it from the heat and apply a thin coating of oil: just a few drops spread out with a paper towel. (Heating the skillet to dry it warms the oil and makes it easier to spread thinly, but as an alternative, you can dry the skillet by wiping it with a paper towel and then apply the oil.) Once your skillet builds up a good level of seasoning, you may be able to skip applying a thin coating of oil each time.

America, Late-19th-Early 20th Century	Europe, 1914-1918	America, 1930s

Skillets on the DL

Cast-iron pattern makers were craftsmen and often carved small, unique figures into their work (the "maker's mark") to identify their work. Companies produced "unmarked" cast iron to save face—they could sell pots in hardware and department stores at lower prices without sacrificing credibility.

Skillets Save Lives!

During World War I, pilots would sometimes sit on skillets to protect themselves from ground fire. Only after development of aircraft armor began in 1918 was this noble cooking implement honorably discharged so it could return to its duties in the kitchen.

A Penny for Your Pots

In order to survive the Great Depression, Lodge Manufacturing, one of the leading cast-iron skillet manufacturers, created a separate catalog of novelty items for rich customers that included cast-iron garden gnomes and painted doorstops in the shape of dogs.

Salvaging Cast Iron

Occasionally, cast iron loses its luster. Rust may creep in. We're not looking to assign blame here, but I'll assume it wasn't your fault. Your head was turned. You were out of town. At worst, you were distracted from utter devotion to your cast-iron skillet by something that happened in life—like, you know, life. Or maybe you've found a piece of vintage cast iron. It is not cracked or damaged beyond repair, but it is in need of some love.

Here's the good news: Where there is rust, there is still hope. Remove the rusted areas with a scouring pad. It's okay to use something harsher than you would ordinarily use, such as steel wool, because you will be rebuilding the skillet's seasoning. Wash the skillet with mild soap and water. As with the steel wool, a little soap is okay in this instance, too, because you will be rehabilitating the skillet later. Dry the skillet thoroughly and then start reseasoning it. Expect that it might take a few rounds of seasoning to return the skillet to good working order. And, as with many skillets, it could be a work in progress for a bit.

Useful Tools

Oven Mitts

Part of the beauty of a skillet made solely of cast iron is that it is equally comfortable atop the stove and in the oven. In either place, the handle of the skillet can get very hot. When you're cooking with the skillet, it's best to approach the skillet assuming that it is hot enough to burn you.

I prefer silicone mitts to cloth. Any mitt is better than none, but cloth mitts can pose risks when even a little wet. The water transfers the heat from the skillet to your skin—which is not ideal, to say the least.

One tip: If you're working on the stovetop and the skillet is still hot, get in the habit of leaving the mitt on the handle.

| 1950s-1960s | America, Late 20th Century | America, Early 1990s |

An Artist's Touch

Skillets are often marked with numbers and letters to indicate size and design. Some of the most interesting model designations from the late 1950s and early 1960s included: AT = Ash Tray Skillet; CP = Cactus Pan; NTP = No Trump Card Pan; and PP = Perch Pan.

Skillets for Sport

Skillet-throwing developed into a popular small-town field day event. In Vermont, the Ladies' Underhanded Skillet Toss soared in popularity; in Iowa, the National Skillet Throwing Contest aimed at scarecrows.

Do You Want Fries with That?

New slang: Home skillet, n. Friend, pal, someone from the same hometown or neighborhood.

Spatula (Plastic or Metal)

The skillet's seasoning is durable, but sometimes even a seasoned skillet feels a little vulnerable, you know? Scratches from a metal spatula are nothing that can't be fixed with time and attention, but going easy on a newly seasoned skillet with a plastic spatula is probably a good idea, at least at first. Once the seasoning has improved, feel free to use metal utensils. In fact, a metal utensil may help smooth out some rough spots in a skillet with a very thick layer of seasoning.

Trivet

Not every surface can handle the heat of the cast-iron skillet right off the stovetop or out of the oven. It helps to have a landing spot handy for the skillet, whether in the form of a countertop you know is safe for the hot skillet or a trivet designed to take the heat. Trivets are also useful for serving. They can protect your table from scratches and the heat of a warm skillet. Silicone and wood trivets are both good options.

Cooling Rack

Trivets and stovetops can be useful as immediate landing spots for a hot skillet. But for cooling, it's best to use a wire rack so that air can circulate around the whole skillet. Look for one made of just metal. Plastic and plastic coatings may suffer under the high temperature of a hot skillet.

Recipe Notes

Ingredients and Measurement

There are so many variables in cooking and baking (the temperature in the room, the calibration of the oven, the power of the stovetop burners); it's good to control the ones we can. A lot of this means carefully selecting and measuring ingredients. I'm almost rolling my eyes at myself now, because I know how this might sound. ("It's not enough that the guy wrote the recipe? He has to write a whole section about how to measure flour, for crying out loud?")

Late 1990s	Early 2000s	America, 2016
Seasoned for Survival	**Numbers Game**	**Too Hot to Handle**
Part of the resurgence in cast iron's popularity was thanks to doomsday preppers, who stuck the cast-iron skillet on their must-have survival lists.	For antique cast-iron collectibles, skillet size is a factor in price. The numbers 8 and 9 were widely produced, but bigger and smaller skillets are rarities. Number 13, an awkward size that is too large for a family but too small for a dinner party, can go for $2,000.	Little has changed in cast-iron technology since the skillet first arrived on the scene. But in 2016, brothers Stephen and Chris Muscarella launched a $1.6-million Kickstarter campaign to produce a high-quality skillet that weighs less than a 13-inch MacBook Pro.

I write this not so much to lay down the law (I won't be popping out of your cupboard to chastise you on your flour measurement or lurking in your refrigerator to read your butter labels) but to establish a common language and a starting point. If you want to start out on the best footing, or you find things not working out to your liking, these are some of the things to consider.

FLOUR

Flour measurement is tricky because it can vary tremendously. It would be a lot easier if we just weighed it, but scales aren't in every kitchen and cup measurements are still very much the standard in the United States. A cup of flour can weigh 4 ounces, 5 ounces, or more, depending on how it's measured. (That's a 25 percent difference in just a single ingredient!) The flour in these recipes was measured using the scoop-and-sweep method. What does this mean? It means the measuring cup is dipped in the flour until overflowing, then the excess flour is leveled off with a knife run straight across the top of the cup, with the excess falling back into the flour container.

EGGS

The recipes in this book call for large eggs. Medium-size or extra-large eggs can run 10 percent bigger or smaller. This may not have much bearing on a recipe with just one egg, but the impact of different size eggs starts to multiply when more are called for in a recipe.

BUTTER

For my money, there is nothing better than salted butter for finishing and serving a dish, but when it comes to baking and cooking, salted butter introduces an unwelcome variable: Salt content can vary. This may not only affect the taste of the finished product—it would, of course, be more or less salty—but in recipes that involve yeast it could make a difference in how much the dough rises, since salt helps keep yeast in check and regulates rising.

YEAST

The recipes in this book call for instant dry yeast, which not only acts quickly but is less fussy in that it can be added directly to dry ingredients. Active dry yeast, on the other hand, typically must first be added to wet ingredients to rehydrate before it's combined with other ingredients.

BAKING POWDER AND BAKING SODA

This might sound like a notion that exists only within the pages of cookbooks, but it's true: Baking powder does not last forever. I mean, it's a room-temperature powder, so it doesn't spoil or disintegrate. But it stops working. And here's the crazy part: It may be as soon as six months after opening that it becomes less effective. Have you ever kept baking powder longer than six months? Of course you have. Fortunately, there's an easy way to see if your baking powder still packs a punch: Drop a big pinch in a bowl and follow it with a splash of boiling water. It should bubble vigorously. If it doesn't, it's time for new baking powder. Regardless, I make a habit of replacing mine every year on my birthday. You might consider doing the same. (Use your own birthday, though—easier to remember.)

Baking soda generally has a longer shelf life, but because it's inexpensive, it can be replaced along with the baking powder. The contents of the old box need not be wasted. I demote it to stove-scrubbing duty: Just mix a little water until it forms a paste and use it to remove baked-on gunk.

SALT

Few things are more elemental to the taste of a dish than proper seasoning, which at its most basic level means the right amount of salt. The recipes in this book use table salt because it's the salt that most people have on hand. It's a fine-grain salt that varies little in the size of its crystals, and that's key for consistent measurement. Kosher or coarse salts are particularly nice for a finishing touch on a dish, but the crystal size can vary a lot between brands, to say nothing of the difference between kosher salt and table salt.

Example: A single tablespoon of standard table salt can equal about 2 tablespoons of one brand of kosher salt or 1½ tablespoons of another. That variability is not your friend when you're trying to measure something for a recipe, so with a few noted exceptions I've stuck to table salt in this book—though of course when it comes to finishing or seasoning to taste, there's no problem using any kind you'd like.

Preparation

Here are two solid pieces of advice: Before making a recipe, read it through to the end. There's nothing like finding out that the final step of a recipe requires a melon baller (that is just an example; nothing in this book requires a melon baller!) and realizing your melon baller is in the shop.

The same applies to ingredients. It's not enough to look in the fridge and know that you have, say, *some* butter to make a recipe. At a certain point in the recipe, you will be forced to confront whether you have *enough* butter. There's *some* butter and there's *enough* butter, and the former is not a good substitute for the latter.

CHAPTER 2

Breakfast and Brunch

Toast with Olive Oil and Tomato

Time: 10 minutes
Yield: Serves 1

I've never owned a toaster—but that has not stopped me from eating toasted bread.

I fell in love with the marriage of crusty bread, ripe tomato, and fruity extra-virgin olive oil in Spain, where the combination crops up as a breakfast and as a snack. This dish was a way to bring part of Spain back with me.

When it comes to toasting bread, yes, a toaster works. Sometimes. But cramming a baguette with olive oil into a toaster seems like a bad idea. (It is; don't try it.) The skillet is the way to develop that golden, oil-toasted crust on a beautiful slice of baguette.

Such a simple recipe puts heavy emphasis on the quality of the ingredients. Use a crusty, rustic loaf for the sliced bread, choose a flavorful extra-virgin olive oil, and select salt with enough bulk to provide crunchy little bursts of salinity. All of those ingredients are available year round. The tomato may be trickier. I often can bring myself to make this only in the summer, when the pleasure of a ripe local tomato is second to none. But sometimes I cave. I'm not made of steel—er, cast iron.

INGREDIENTS

2 tablespoons extra-virgin olive oil, plus more for serving

1 (5-inch) piece baguette, sliced lengthwise

1 ripe medium-size tomato, sliced about ½-inch thick

¼ teaspoon coarse sea salt (see Note)

NOTE

- *Use the coarsest salt you can find, since it adds not only flavor but also crunch.*

1 Preheat the skillet over medium heat for 2 minutes.

2 Add the olive oil to the skillet and let the oil warm for about 30 seconds before adding the bread, cut side down. Press the bread down slightly to help it soak up the oil and make contact with the skillet.

3 Cook until the surface is golden brown, about 3 minutes.

4 Remove the bread from the skillet and place it, toasted side up, on a serving plate. Drizzle with more olive oil to taste. Place the tomato slices on the baguette, sprinkle evenly with salt, and serve.

A well-seasoned skillet will last a lifetime.

Egg in a Basket

It's the evolution of bread toasted in the skillet, wherein the egg is fried in the center.

Time: 10 minutes
Yield: Serves 1

There are a lot of names for this—UFO, toad in a hole, egg in a frame, hole in one. You could be sitting down to breakfast before we got through the whole list of names, so we'll just settle on Egg in a Basket and specify that it's a whole egg cooked in a golden, buttery piece of bread with its center removed.

That center piece of bread—and pay attention, because this is the best part—is also toasted in butter in the skillet. Some people eat the egg and its surrounding toast first. Others, correctly, figure that life is short and uncertain and head straight for that buttery circle of toast while it's still almost too hot (as though there were such a thing when it involves things coated in butter).

Cooking an egg on cast iron is a real test of the skillet's seasoning. Those lucky enough to have a well-seasoned skillet will find that the egg releases easily. Others may find it takes a little more butter (see Note).

I still remember the summer morning when my fried egg slid off my skillet as though it was on rails. The clouds parted and a ray of light shone upon my skillet.

No? I may have embellished. The egg thing is true, though.

INGREDIENTS

1 slice sandwich bread

2 teaspoons salted butter, softened (see Tip)

1 large egg

Salt and freshly ground black pepper

NOTE

- *Frying an egg in your cast-iron skillet is one of the surest tests of its seasoning. If your skillet is anything less than thoroughly nonstick, count on melting an additional 1/2 teaspoon butter in the center of the bread in Step 4 before the egg hits the skillet.*

1 Preheat the skillet over medium heat for 2 minutes.

2 While the skillet heats, spread each side of the bread with 1 teaspoon of butter.

3 Use a cup with a mouth about 2½ inches in diameter to cut a hole out of the center of the bread by pressing into the bread while twisting the cup back and forth. Remove the circle of bread from the center and place both pieces in the skillet.

4 Crack the egg into a ramekin or small cup, then pour it into the center of the bread. (Cracking the egg first into a ramekin helps you control how it lands in the skillet and gives you a line of defense against errant eggshells.)

5 Cook until the bread is golden brown, about 2 minutes. (Check the circle of bread; with no egg, it's easier.)

6 Use a spatula to flip both pieces of bread, and continue to cook until the bread is golden brown, about 2 minutes.

7 Remove the bread and egg from the skillet, sprinkle the egg with salt and pepper to taste, and serve.

Variation
Garnish with chopped fresh chives or dill sprinkled on the egg.

TIP
- **To soften butter quickly, cut it into small pieces and press down on the pieces with your (clean!) thumb. Your body heat will warm the butter. Or use a vegetable peeler to shave off thin ribbons, which will come quickly to room temperature.**

Egg in a Basket, page 19

French-Toasted Waffles

Time: 20 minutes
Yield: Serves 2

No longer do you have to choose between two favorites. It's breakfast for the indecisive!

I have a history with waffles. I wrote a whole book on unexpected recipes for your waffle iron and made a point of including a mere two recipes for actual waffles (which I call "waffled waffle batter"). I spent a lot of time explaining to people that while that book was about what to make in the waffle iron, it was really about anything *but* conventional waffles.

I have nothing against waffles! In fact, I double the recipe when I make them, even if I'm only cooking for myself. The leftovers go straight into the freezer, where they await a second life. Sure, sometimes I simply warm them in the oven. But sometimes I French-toast them, and the skillet is the perfect vessel for that. Is it possible to make waffles in your skillet? No. But it's possible to make them *better*.

I'm happy to say that this works with thicker, Belgian-style waffles *and* the thinner ones in your grocer's freezer case that you don't want to, um, "let go." And you barely have to thaw them first.

INGREDIENTS

2 large eggs

1/2 cup milk

1/4 teaspoon vanilla extract

Pinch of salt

4 frozen waffles (store-bought or homemade; thin or Belgian-style; see Note)

Unsalted butter, for greasing the skillet

Maple syrup and salted butter, for serving

- *The waffles shouldn't be frozen solid when you start, but they don't need to be completely thawed, either. Most store-bought waffles will thaw sufficiently in the time it takes to preheat the skillet and combine the other ingredients. Homemade waffles are likely denser and may take more time; it's better to let them thaw about 15 minutes before you start.*

1 Preheat the skillet over medium-low heat for 2 minutes.

2 While the skillet heats, whisk together the eggs, milk, vanilla, and salt in a pie pan or baking dish.

3 Place 1 waffle in the egg mixture and soak it until it has absorbed some of the liquid. A thin waffle may only need a quick dip; a thicker one may need about 30 seconds. Flip the waffle with a fork and soak the other side.

4 Melt about 1 teaspoon unsalted butter in the skillet. Use the fork to pick up the waffle, and allow excess batter to drip off, tilting the waffle if necessary for the liquid to escape the nooks and crannies.

5 Place the waffle in the skillet and cook it until golden brown, about 2 minutes. (Thicker Belgian-style waffles require as much as an extra minute.) Use a spatula to flip it, and cook until the other side is golden brown, about 2 minutes. (Again, allow another minute for thicker waffles.)

6 Serve the first waffle immediately or keep it warm in an oven preheated to its lowest temperature. Repeat Steps 3 through 5 with the remaining waffles.

7 Serve warm, with maple syrup and butter.

Variation

- *Add ¼ teaspoon ground cinnamon, ¼ teaspoon grated orange zest, or a pinch of ground or freshly grated nutmeg to the batter.*

Chilaquiles

Fried tortillas—from the skillet or from the store—are the key to this shareable and satisfying salsa and cheese concoction.

Time: 1 hour 45 minutes with freshly fried chips; 1 hour with store-bought chips

Yield: Serves 6

This is not a pretentious dish, but it does have a lot to offer, namely tortilla chips, salsa, cheese, and eggs. What more is there, really? It's not exactly a light breakfast, but it is a very satisfying brunch. Fans of brinner—that's breakfast for dinner—might appreciate washing it down with a beer.

You can make or buy tortillas and fry them into chips, or start with store-bought chips. It's the same for the salsa: Make your own or open a jar.

There are multiple paths to chilaquiles—and they all run through the skillet.

INGREDIENTS

Neutral-flavored oil (such as canola or peanut) for frying and 15 (5-inch) corn tortillas (page 59 or store-bought) or 8 ounces unsalted tortilla chips

2 cups Charred Tomato Salsa (page 70) or store-bought chipotle-tomato salsa

2 cups reduced-sodium chicken broth

Salt and freshly ground black pepper

4 large eggs, lightly beaten

2 cups shredded cheese (such as Cheddar, Monterey Jack, or Chihuahua)

Sour cream or Mexican crema and finely chopped scallion greens, for serving

NOTE

• *The tortillas will fry up better if they're slightly dry. Leave them out of the package for a few hours before frying. Or place them on a baking sheet in the oven for 5 minutes as it preheats. If you're starting with tortilla chips, preheat the oven, then skip to Step 5.*

1 Preheat the oven to 350°F with one rack in the middle.

2 Heat about ¾ inch oil to 350°F in the skillet over medium heat. For safety's sake, do not fill the skillet with oil beyond its halfway point. Do not allow the oil to smoke. If that happens, carefully move the skillet off the heat. While the oil heats, tear each tortilla into 5 or 6 pieces. When the oil is hot enough for frying, a small piece of tortilla in the skillet will sizzle immediately.

3 Cover a large plate with paper towels. Place the tortilla pieces in the skillet without crowding them and fry until they are just crisp, 1 to 2 minutes, depending on the thickness of the tortillas. Remove the chips with a slotted spoon and place them on the plate to drain. Repeat until all of the chips are fried.

4 Remove the skillet from the heat and transfer it to a rack to cool slightly before pouring off the oil. (See Tip for details on saving the oil.)

5 Place the skillet over medium-high heat and add the salsa and chicken broth. Bring to a boil, then turn the heat to medium low and cook until about half of the liquid has evaporated, about 20 minutes. Taste to check for seasoning and add salt and pepper as necessary.

6 Remove the skillet from the heat and stir in the eggs and cheese. Add the tortilla chips, using a spoon or spatula to mix everything thoroughly, coating the chips with the salsa-and-egg mixture. Stirring will become easier as the chips absorb the liquid and become more pliable.

7 Place the skillet in the oven and bake until the cheese is melted and any visible chips are golden brown, about 20 minutes.

8 Remove the skillet from the oven and transfer it to a rack to cool slightly, about 10 minutes. Serve warm, with sour cream and scallions. Leftovers can be refrigerated in a covered container for up to 2 days.

Variation

- *Add 1 cup black beans or chopped cooked chicken, turkey, beef, or pork at the end of Step 6.*

TIP

- **Save and reuse your frying oil! Strain it through cheesecloth, a coffee filter, or a fine sieve. Store in the refrigerator in a sealed container for up to 3 months. As you reuse the oil, it will not tolerate high temperatures as well, and the amount of time it can be stored will decrease. It's generally okay to use oil once or twice more after the initial frying. If you've used it more than three times, or stored it more than 3 months, or if the oil has turned cloudy or has an "off" scent, discard it in a sealed container in the garbage.**

Chilaquiles, page 25

Apple-Sour Cream Skillet-Size Pancake

Time: 45 minutes
Yield: Serves 6

With this pancake, everyone's breakfast is ready at the same time.

I hate to speak ill of the pancake, but there is at least one obvious disadvantage: If you're cooking for more than one person, it's hard to have everyone's food ready at once. And heaven help the person actually making the pancakes. I have to—I mean, *he or she has to*—either eat standing up while preparing the rest of the pancakes or wait until the end of the process as the danger of being "hangry" creeps upward. (Keeping pancakes warm in the oven is not so bad, but it's no one's vision of ideal.)

So, yes, you can make conventional pancakes in your skillet. It's great for that.

But a skillet-size pancake may be a better idea for anyone not dining solo.

This version, sometimes called a German apple pancake or a Dutch baby, may suffer from an apparent confusion of national identity, but everything else about it is quite straightforward. In particular, the way it comes together in the skillet is a thing of beauty: The sweetened apples caramelize slightly on the stovetop, then the batter is added and the whole assembly is placed in the oven to finish.

Breakfast is ready for everyone at the same time. And the race is on for seconds.

INGREDIENTS

¾ cup unbleached all-purpose flour

5 tablespoons granulated sugar

¼ teaspoon salt

¾ cup milk

¼ cup sour cream

3 large eggs

1 teaspoon vanilla extract

¼ teaspoon ground cinnamon

Pinch of ground or freshly grated nutmeg

4 tablespoons (½ stick) unsalted butter

4 medium-size tart apples (such as Granny Smith, Cortland, Jonathan, and/ or Northern Spy; about 1½ pounds), peeled, quartered, and sliced about ¼-inch thick

Confectioners' sugar, for garnish

1 Preheat the oven to 450°F with one rack in the middle.

2 In a medium-size bowl, whisk together the flour, 1 tablespoon of the granulated sugar, and the salt. Add the milk, sour cream, eggs, and vanilla and whisk until just combined. A few lumps are okay.

3 In a small bowl, combine the cinnamon, nutmeg, and the remaining 4 tablespoons granulated sugar.

4 Preheat the skillet over medium heat for 2 minutes.

5 Melt the butter in the skillet, then add the apples. Sprinkle with the spiced sugar and cook, stirring, until the apples have softened and the liquid in the skillet turns syrupy, 5 to 10 minutes.

6 Remove the skillet from the heat, pour the batter evenly over the apples, and place the skillet in the oven. Cook until the pancake is puffed and golden brown around the edges, about 25 minutes.

7 Remove the skillet from the oven and transfer it to a rack to cool slightly, about 10 minutes. The pancake will deflate as it cools. Slice the pancake into wedges and dust each wedge with confectioners' sugar just before serving. Leftovers can be refrigerated in a covered container for up to 2 days.

Big Berry Muffin

Time: 1 hour
Cool: 1 hour
Yield: 8 wedges

Your skillet stands in for a muffin tin, giving you a pan-size muffin perfect for slicing and serving warm with a pat of salted butter.

Asking what separates a muffin from a cupcake might be the baking equivalent of asking how many angels can dance on the head of a pin. In the first place, it depends on who's answering the question. But more importantly, answering the question is time you could spend making muffins.

One bite of a warm slice and you will no longer care how many angels can dance on the head of a muffin—if that was ever the question—though you may hear a choir of angels well up in your head as the rich crumble topping joins the moist muffin and slightly tart bursts of fruit in your mouth.

INGREDIENTS

Topping

1/2 cup unbleached all-purpose flour

2 tablespoons firmly packed light brown sugar

2 tablespoons granulated sugar

1/2 teaspoon baking powder

Pinch of salt

3 tablespoons cold unsalted butter, cut into cubes

Muffin

1/2 cup milk

1 large egg plus 1 large egg yolk

1 teaspoon vanilla extract

1 1/2 cups unbleached all-purpose flour, plus 2 teaspoons for coating the berries

1/2 cup granulated sugar

1 1/2 teaspoons baking powder

3/4 teaspoon salt

8 tablespoons (1 stick) unsalted butter, melted and cooled (see Notes)

2 cups frozen mixed berries (see Notes)

Salted butter, softened, for serving

NOTES

- *Melt the butter in the skillet and avoid dirtying another dish: Place the skillet over low heat and add the butter in small chunks. Let sit until almost all the butter has melted, about 2 minutes, then remove the skillet from the heat. Stopping before all the butter melts allows the residual heat to fully melt it, and allows it all to cool more quickly. Any residual butter can stay in the skillet.*

- *Most berries can be used, alone or in combination. Blackberries, blueberries, or raspberries work particularly nicely. Avoid strawberries, which release too much water as they cook. Use the berries straight from the freezer and don't skip coating them in flour—it keeps their color from running too much in the muffin.*

1. Preheat the oven to 350°F with one rack in the middle.

2. Make the topping: In a small bowl, using your fingers or a fork, work the flour, brown sugar, granulated sugar, baking powder, and salt into the butter until everything is evenly distributed and few large chunks of butter remain. Set aside.

3. Make the muffin: In a measuring cup, whisk together the milk, egg, egg yolk, and vanilla with a fork.

4. In a large bowl, whisk together 1½ cups flour, the granulated sugar, baking powder, and salt. Add the milk mixture and melted butter. Use a spatula to fold both into the flour. A few streaks or lumps of flour are okay. Toss the berries with the remaining 2 teaspoons flour and fold into the batter, distributing them evenly.

5. Pour the batter into the skillet, spread it evenly with a spatula, and sprinkle with the topping. Bake until the topping is golden brown and a toothpick inserted in the center of the muffin comes out clean, 45 to 50 minutes.

6. Remove the skillet from the oven and transfer it to a rack to cool until just warm, about 1 hour. Slice and serve with salted butter. Leftovers can be stored for 1 day at room temperature in the skillet, covered loosely with plastic wrap. Slices can be wrapped in plastic wrap and frozen in a zip-top bag for up to 3 months.

Variation

- *Use fresh berries: Two 6-ounce packages of berries yield about 2 cups. Wash and dry the berries thoroughly and toss them in 1 tablespoon flour. (Fresh berries need a little more flour than frozen to account for their extra moisture.) In Step 4, it's okay if the berries break up a bit as you fold them into the batter. The muffin will bake more quickly; check it after 40 minutes.*

Big Berry Muffin, page 31

Sausage, Cheddar, and Broccoli Strata

Your skillet offers up layer after layer of something to love in this oven-to-table casserole.

Time: 1 hour 20 minutes, plus overnight resting

Yield: Serves 6

One of the huge advantages of a strata is the make-ahead component. Most of the work can be done the night before. In the morning, all that's left to do is layer the ingredients in the skillet and bake.

Many strata recipes call for the ingredients to be layered the night before and stored in the pan in which they're baked, but that's not ideal for the skillet. (The dampness of the ingredients and the refrigerator could lead to rust.)

You *could* just toss all of the ingredients together in one bowl and pour them out into the skillet—though "strata" means layers, so technically once you've lost the layers, you've lost the strata. Besides, it's easy enough to refrigerate the ingredients separately and then bring them together in the skillet just before baking.

The only thing left to figure out is who wakes up and puts it in the oven. But this is a cookbook. I can't help you with that.

INGREDIENTS

4 large eggs

1¾ cups milk

¼ cup freshly grated Parmesan cheese

¼ teaspoon salt

¼ teaspoon freshly ground black pepper

1 small baguette (8 ounces), sliced ½-inch thick (about 5 cups)

8 ounces Italian sausage, casings removed

2 cups chopped broccoli (about 1 small stalk, florets and stem)

1 small white or yellow onion, chopped

2 tablespoons olive oil

1 cup shredded Cheddar cheese

1. In a large bowl, whisk together the eggs, milk, Parmesan, salt, and pepper. Add the bread and cover. Allow the bread to soak while you proceed with the recipe, mixing occasionally so that the egg mixture is absorbed.

2. Preheat the skillet over medium-high heat for 2 minutes. Add the sausage, broccoli, and onion, breaking up the sausage with a spatula or fork. Cook until the sausage is cooked through, the broccoli is bright green, and the onion is soft, about 7 minutes.

3. Keeping the bread mixture covered, refrigerate it overnight. In a separate covered container, refrigerate the sausage mixture.

4. The next day, preheat the oven to 350°F with one rack in the middle.

5. Swirl the olive oil in the skillet to coat the bottom and sides evenly. Place half of the bread-and-egg mixture in the bottom of the skillet. Sprinkle with half of the sausage mixture, then with half of the Cheddar. Finish the layers with the remaining ingredients in the same order.

6. Bake until the cheese is browned and any visible bread is golden brown, about 1 hour.

7. Remove the skillet from the oven and transfer it to a rack to cool slightly, about 10 minutes, before serving. Leftovers can be refrigerated in a covered container for up to 2 days.

TIP

- **Don't want to wait overnight? While the sausage and vegetables are cooking, stir and press down the bread mixture frequently to make sure the liquid is absorbed.**

Giant Cinnamon Bun

Enjoy this skillet-size bun warm from the oven, just right for a weekend breakfast or brunch with friends.

Time: 2 hours 15 minutes

Cool: 30 minutes

Yield: Serves 8

Adapting cinnamon buns for the skillet had to mean more than just creating an outsize version of the original. This was a chance to take it in a new direction. My goal here was to create pleasing geometry when the bun is viewed in the skillet, and to offer up beautiful cross sections when the whole thing is cut for serving.

Here, the dough is slathered with butter and sugar, then rolled up and coiled again. This layering and coiling means that in the skillet, the Giant Cinnamon Bun looks like a large version of your favorite cinnamon bun. Then it gets better: Cutting into it reveals more layers of butter, cinnamon, and sugar swirled inside.

INGREDIENTS

Dough

1 cup milk (see Note)

1 large egg

2½ cups unbleached all-purpose flour, plus more for kneading and rolling

2 tablespoons granulated sugar

1½ teaspoons instant yeast

1 teaspoon salt

Nonstick cooking spray or neutral-flavored oil (such as canola or peanut)

Filling

⅓ cup firmly packed light brown sugar

⅓ cup granulated sugar

1 tablespoon ground cinnamon

8 tablespoons (1 stick) unsalted butter, melted

Icing

1 cup confectioners' sugar

2 tablespoons milk, plus more if needed

½ teaspoon vanilla extract

- *Use whole milk if available. It adds richness to the dough.*

1 Make the dough: Measure the milk in a measuring cup, then use a fork to beat in the egg.

2 In a large bowl, using a wooden spoon, or in the bowl of a stand mixer fitted with the dough hook, combine the flour, sugar, yeast, and salt. Add the milk mixture and stir to combine.

3 If using a mixer, knead the dough on low speed for 5 minutes. If kneading by hand, dust a work surface lightly with flour, turn out the dough onto it, and knead for about 10 minutes. The dough should be tacky to the touch, smooth, and no longer ragged.

4 Spray a large bowl with cooking spray or wipe it with a thin coat of oil. Shape the dough into a ball and place it in the bowl. Cover tightly with a lid or plastic wrap and let rise at room temperature for 1 hour, until almost doubled in bulk.

5 While the dough rises, make the cinnamon sugar filling: In a small bowl, mix the brown sugar, granulated sugar, and cinnamon.

6 Preheat the oven to 350°F with one rack in the middle.

7 Dust a work surface lightly with flour, turn out the dough onto it, dust the top with flour, and use a rolling pin to roll it into a circle about 14 inches in diameter, adding flour as necessary on the top and bottom to prevent sticking. Give the dough an occasional quarter turn or flip it over while you roll to help prevent sticking and produce a more even circle.

8 Brush off the excess flour, then brush about half of the butter evenly onto the dough. Reserve about 2 tablespoons of the cinnamon sugar and sprinkle the rest atop the butter.

9 Roll up the dough in a tight log, pinch along the seam to seal it, and turn the dough so that the seam is on the bottom. The center of the log will be thicker than the two ends. Press down gently on the center with your hands to make the thickness more even, then use your hands to gently flatten the top of the log. (The flat surface makes it easier for the butter and sugar to adhere in the next step.)

10 Brush with some of the remaining butter and sprinkle with all of the remaining cinnamon sugar. Start rolling at one end, coiling the dough upward to form a spiral perpendicular to the work surface.

Giant Cinnamon Bun, page 37

11 Turn the spiral so that it is flat on the work surface, then lift it into the skillet. Gently press down with your hands to flatten the spiral until it forms a circle 8 inches in diameter, keeping the outer end of the spiral tucked under.

12 Brush the dough with more of the butter and place the skillet in the oven. Bake until golden brown, about 35 minutes.

13 While the bun bakes, make the icing: In a small bowl, mix the confectioner's sugar, milk, and vanilla. The mixture should be spreadable. If it is not, add more milk 1 tablespoon at a time.

14 Remove the skillet from the oven and transfer it to a rack to cool. If you have butter remaining, brush it across the top of the bun. Let the bun cool for about 30 minutes, until warm but not hot.

15 Drizzle the icing on the bun and serve warm. Leftovers can be stored for 1 day at room temperature in the skillet, covered loosely with plastic wrap. Slices can be wrapped in plastic wrap and frozen in a zip-top freezer bag for up to 3 months.

TIPS

Looking to get a head start? Here are two options.

- **The dough can be made up to Step 4 and stored overnight in the refrigerator. Remove it from the refrigerator 1 hour before proceeding.**

- **Prepare the dough through Step 11 (skip preheating the oven). Instead of lifting it into the skillet, spray a large plate with nonstick cooking spray, place the shaped dough on the plate, spray the top, and cover it with plastic wrap. Store it overnight in the refrigerator. When you're ready to bake, place the dough in the skillet and let it stand 30 minutes while the oven preheats. Pick up at Step 12.**

Crepes with Raspberries and Mascarpone

Time: 1 hour 30 minutes

Yield: 12 stuffed crepes

Can you buy a crepe pan? Sure. Or you can use the skillet you already have.

C repes are not particularly difficult to make, but they do have a French name so that automatically registers them a step up from pancakes in certain circles.

You can buy them premade in the supermarket and, yes, that's totally fine. But sometimes you *want* someone to know that you went through the trouble of making something, and sometimes cooking is a little bit of theater, and sometimes on a Saturday morning it's nice to be able to casually toss out the word "crepe" as though you lived like this every day and—*what?*—*why, it would certainly be no trouble at all to whip up a batch!*

Well, would you look at that—you even have raspberries and mascarpone in the refrigerator! (I mean, you're not a savage, so of course you do.) I *suppose* those will go splendidly with the crepes for a casual weekend breakfast, you say casually.

And they will.

How do you take your coffee?

Crepes with Raspberries and Mascarpone, page 41

INGREDIENTS

Filling

8 ounces mascarpone, softened

1 tablespoon granulated sugar

1/2 teaspoon vanilla extract

Crepes

1 cup unbleached all-purpose flour

Pinch of salt

1 tablespoon granulated sugar

1 1/4 cups milk (see Note)

2 large eggs

2 tablespoons unsalted butter, melted and cooled

Fresh raspberries and confectioners' sugar, for garnish

NOTE

* *Use whole milk if available. It's what the French would use and I'm inclined to defer to them on crepes.*

1 Make the filling: In a small bowl, use a hand-held mixer or whisk to whip the mascarpone, sugar, and vanilla until well combined and fluffy. Set aside.

2 Make the crepes: In a medium-size bowl or large measuring cup with a spout for easier pouring, whisk together the flour, salt, and sugar. In another medium-size bowl, whisk the milk, eggs, and butter. Add the flour mixture gradually, whisking as you go, until the batter is smooth. Allow the batter to rest in the refrigerator for 1 hour.

3 Preheat the skillet over medium heat for 2 minutes.

4 If the batter has separated, whisk to recombine. Add about 1 teaspoon butter to the skillet and spread it around with a silicone brush or spatula.

5 Add about 3 tablespoons of the batter to the skillet, swirling it around so that the bottom of the skillet is coated (see Tip on swirling).

6 Cook until the top is dry, about 1 minute, then loosen the crepe with a spatula and flip it to cook the other side until just brown in spots, another 20 to 30 seconds. Earlier crepes may take longer to cook than later ones. Turn down the heat if you notice they are browning too quickly. Do not allow crepes to become crispy; they should be soft and pliable.

7 Transfer the cooked crepe to a plate and repeat Steps 4 through 6 with the remaining batter, adding about 1 teaspoon butter only as necessary to keep skillet greased.

8 For each crepe, if one side of your crepe is more attractive than the other, start with the more presentable side down. Place 1 tablespoon of the filling just off the center of the crepe. Fold the crepe in half and then in half again to make a triangle, keeping the filling in the tip.

9 Garnish each crepe with 2 or 3 raspberries, sprinkle with confectioners' sugar, and serve warm or at room temperature.

TIPS

- **On swirling the batter: Becoming a practiced swirler can take a few tries. You might find it easier to lift the skillet off the heat with one hand while pouring in the batter with the other hand. Begin to swirl as soon as the batter hits the skillet. (Keeping the skillet off the heat allows the batter to stay liquid and flow more easily for a bit longer.) Once the batter has spread out, place the skillet back on the heat. The whole process takes longer to read about than it does to do; about 10 seconds should pass between the time the batter first hits the skillet and the time it has spread out.**

Variations

- *For a lighter filling, use an equal amount of Greek yogurt in place of the mascarpone, and add a drizzle of honey instead of a sprinkle of confectioner's sugar.*

- *Use fresh blueberries or sliced strawberries instead of raspberries.*

- **Is your first crepe too crisp? Does it look a bit too much like abstract art? That happens to everyone. It's what we call a practice crepe. It's for the dog.**

- **The batter and filling can be made one day ahead, covered, and stored in the refrigerator. Whisk the batter to recombine, and allow the filling to come to room temperature before proceeding.**

- **The crepes can be made one day ahead and stored, covered, in the refrigerator. Reheat briefly in the skillet over low heat before assembling.**

Toasted Spice Mixes
Gomashio, Toasted Cumin, and Za'atar

A hot, dry skillet is the perfect vessel for bringing out the flavor of spices.

GOMASHIO
Time: 10 minutes
Yield: 1 cup

TOASTED CUMIN
Time: 10 minutes
Yield: About ¼ cup

ZA'ATAR
Time: 20 minutes
Yield: About ¼ cup

Whole spices take on new dimensions when toasted, but if you don't have a particularly powerful food processor or spice grinder, you can also toast ground spices.

Toasting spices requires a dry skillet—it's worth giving the skillet a quick wipe with a paper towel to make sure it's absolutely dry before starting.

Toasting happens quickly and isn't a process that can be reversed. (Thus, it's better to toast cautiously.) The idea is to make these spice mixes and hold on to them for weeks or months. Burned spices aren't something you'll want to hold on to, so use your nose and your eyes to keep tabs on the spices' progress in the skillet—and don't walk away from the stove.

Gomashio (Sesame Seed Seasoning Mix)

This simple mixture, sometimes spelled *gomasio*, can be sprinkled atop popcorn, rice, fish, chicken, beef, tofu, sliced cucumber, or steamed vegetables.

INGREDIENTS

1 cup unroasted, unhulled sesame seeds

2 teaspoons coarse salt

NOTES

- *Unroasted, unhulled sesame seeds are often available in health food stores. Unroasted hulled sesame seeds may be substituted; toasting time may be shorter.*

- *Coarse salt provides little bursts of salinity and texture throughout the mix. If you have only ordinary table salt, reduce the salt to 1 teaspoon and add more to taste, one generous pinch at a time.*

1 Preheat the skillet over medium-low heat for 2 minutes.

2 Toast the sesame seeds, stirring frequently, until they begin to turn fragrant, about 5 minutes. Keep a close eye on them; they will burn if you let them. Once the sesame seeds are fragrant, pour them onto a plate or into a bowl to stop the toasting.

3 Pour the sesame seeds into a food processor, mortar, or spice grinder. Add the salt and grind until most seeds are broken down and the mixture resembles sand. Stop before the mixture becomes powdery or turns to a paste.

4 Store in a covered glass container in a cool dry place for up to several weeks, or in the refrigerator for up to several months. Any off smell from the sesame seeds' natural oil turning rancid means it is time to toss the gomashio.

Variation

- *Add toasted seaweed (such as nori) to the mix. Add one handful, grind, then sample the mix before adding more.*

Toasted Cumin Seasoning Mix

Keep it tableside to sprinkle on corn on the cob, mix into taco fillings, add to sour cream dip, use to season vegetables in Grilled Vegetable and Cheddar Nachos (page 93), or add to Charred Tomato Salsa (page 70).

Grated zest of 2 limes

2 tablespoons cumin seeds

1 tablespoon coarse salt

1 teaspoon freshly ground black pepper

1 teaspoon sweet paprika

1 teaspoon garlic powder

1 teaspoon onion powder

1/2 teaspoon sugar

1/4 teaspoon chili powder, plus more, to taste

1 Preheat the skillet over medium-low heat for 2 minutes.

2 Toast the lime zest and cumin, stirring frequently, until the lime zest is no longer moist and the cumin is fragrant, about 5 minutes.

3 Pour the zest and cumin into a food processor, mortar, or spice grinder. Add the salt, pepper, paprika, garlic powder, onion powder, sugar, and chili powder. Grind until most of the cumin seeds are broken up and the mixture is well blended. Taste and add more chili powder to taste, one small pinch at a time.

4 Store in a covered glass container in a cool dry place for up to several weeks, or in the refrigerator for up to several months.

Za'atar

This mix features sumac, a Middle Eastern spice with a lemony kick. Combine with olive oil for a pita bread dipping sauce, sprinkle over hard-boiled eggs, or dust onto a tomato and cucumber salad.

INGREDIENTS

10 sprigs fresh thyme

2 tablespoons unroasted sesame seeds (hulled or unhulled)

2 teaspoons ground sumac

1/4 teaspoon coarse salt

1 Preheat the oven to 300°F with one rack in the middle.

2 Place the thyme in the skillet and bake until it is dry and the leaves crumble off the sprigs when rubbed between your fingers, about 10 minutes.

3 Remove the skillet from the oven and place it on the stovetop over low heat. Set aside the thyme.

4 Add the sesame seeds to the skillet and toast them, stirring frequently, until they begin to turn fragrant, about 5 minutes.

5 Remove the sesame seeds from the skillet and transfer them to a plate to cool.

6 Remove the thyme leaves from the stems and finely chop them. (You should have about ½ teaspoon.) Combine the thyme with the sesame seeds, sumac, and salt. Taste and add more salt as necessary.

7 Store in a covered glass container in a cool dry place for up to several weeks, or in the refrigerator for up to several months. Any off smell from the sesame seeds' natural oil turning rancid means it is time to toss the za'atar.

A variety of skillets is a luxury, but you need only one.

Popcorn in Clarified Butter

POPCORN
Time: 5 minutes
Yield: Serves 2

CLARIFIED BUTTER
Time: 3 hours
Yield: About ¾ cup

You're going to need to cover the skillet, unless you plan on chasing popped kernels all over the kitchen.

Popcorn topped with butter is one thing. But popcorn *popped* in butter? It's on another level. You may never settle for microwave popcorn again.

It does require some attention: You must shake the skillet to redistribute the kernels as they pop. And to optimize the number of popped kernels and avoid burned popcorn, you must listen to the kernels to know when to stop. But it's all over in three minutes, and paying a little attention is a small price for popcorn this good.

Clarified butter is key here. *But butter is butter, right?* you might be thinking. Yes and no. Butter is butterfat, water, and milk solids. We're really after the pure butterfat, since milk solids can burn at high popcorn-popping temperatures, and the water isn't doing us any favors.

Clarifying butter takes time. The good news is that once you do it, it will keep for eons. No clarified butter? No problem. See the Variations for substitutes. But don't substitute regular, unclarified butter, which will burn.

INGREDIENTS

1 tablespoon clarified butter (recipe follows; or see Variations for alternatives)

¼ cup popping corn

1 tablespoon salted butter, or more, to taste, melted, for serving

1 Melt the clarified butter (or appropriate substitute) in the skillet over low heat, if necessary. Add the popping corn to the butter, cover with aluminum foil or a lid, and turn the heat to high. (A glass lid is handy for allowing you to watch as the corn pops, but it's not necessary.)

2 Tilt the skillet to swirl the kernels and butter as they heat. When the kernels begin to pop, after about 2 minutes, gently shake the skillet continuously until the sound of popping slows, about 1 minute.

3 Remove the skillet from the heat and continue shaking until the popping stops altogether. Taking care because the skillet and cover will be very hot, partially remove the foil to allow the steam to escape for 1 minute.

4 Remove the foil completely and pour the popcorn into a large bowl. Serve hot, tossed with the melted butter.

Variations

- *No clarified butter? Use bacon fat, coconut oil, peanut oil, or corn oil.*

- *Topping options are nearly endless. Try*

  - *Gomashio, page 48*

  - *Salt and freshly ground black pepper*

  - *Extra-virgin olive oil and freshly grated Parmesan cheese*

  - *Extra-virgin olive oil and honey*

Clarified Butter

Clarified butter, also called *ghee*, can withstand much higher temperatures than regular butter without smoking or burning. It also has the added benefit of keeping for months in the refrigerator.

Some methods call for straining the butter in cheesecloth, but that's not something I usually have around. It's much easier to refrigerate it and separate when it's solid.

INGREDIENT

½ pound (2 sticks) unsalted butter, cut into pieces

1 Place the butter in the skillet and heat over low heat until melted, about 15 minutes.

2 Keep the butter at a very low simmer, adjusting the heat if necessary, so that tiny bubbles gently break the surface and foam rises to the top, about 10 minutes.

3 Remove the skillet from the heat, allow the layers to settle for a few minutes, and then skim off the foam with a spoon. (See Tips for suggestions on how to use the foam.)

4 Pour the butter into a glass storage container and allow to stand at room temperature for 30 minutes. Skim off any foam that rises to the top as it settles.

5 Cover and refrigerate until the butterfat is solid, about 2 hours.

6 Remove the butter from the refrigerator. You should see a thin layer of white liquid trapped under a thick layer

Popcorn in Clarified Butter, page 51

of butterfat. Use a dull knife or spoon to cut away a corner of the butterfat to provide a path for the liquid to escape. Pour off and discard that liquid.

7 Store the clarified butter in a covered glass container in the refrigerator. If your clarified butter is grainy, don't worry; that's normal.

TIPS

- **You don't have to throw away the foam that rises to the top! Save it to serve on buttered noodles, stir into your oatmeal, spread on waffles or pancakes—or to top popcorn.**

- **So now you have clarified butter. What else can you do with it? Take advantage of its ability to tolerate high heat and use it to sauté meat or vegetables.**

Some recipes have to be removed from the skillet, but others can be enjoyed right from the pan.

Parmesan Tuiles

Time: 20 minutes
Yield: 4 tuiles

Shredded cheese and a hot skillet give you an elegant garnish or light appetizer.

Tuile means "tile" in French but, more important, can also mean a thin wafer of cookie or, in this case, of cheese. I've seen these beautiful lacey disks sold at the supermarket for a hefty markup over grated cheese, but don't fall into the trap of believing they're difficult to make; they're not. They're often made on a cookie sheet, but you can easily make a small batch in your skillet.

Broken in large pieces for snacking or perched on top of a salad as a garnish, they'll *look* like you spent more time making them than you did.

INGREDIENT

4 tablespoons finely shredded Parmesan cheese (about 1½ ounces)

NOTE

- *Shredded cheese from the supermarket or from a food processor shredding disk works best. Shredding by hand produces shorter strands that have less chance to interlock with other strands and form the lacey pattern you're after.*

1 Preheat the skillet over medium-low heat for 2 minutes.

2 For each tuile, sprinkle 1 tablespoon Parmesan in a circle about 3 inches in diameter. Don't pack the circles too densely; leaving some small holes will give your tuiles their trademark lacey pattern.

3 Cook until the cheese just begins to bubble and turn golden, about 2 minutes, then remove the skillet from the heat and let cool for 10 minutes.

4 Use a spatula to move the tuiles from the skillet onto a flat surface to cool for about 5 minutes.

Parmesan Tuiles, page 55

5 Serve at room temperature as a garnish, on a cheese plate, or on salads.

Variations

- *Use Asiago, Pecorino Romano, or Grana Padano alone or in combination instead of Parmesan.*

- *Add ¼ teaspoon dried thyme or freshly ground black pepper to the cheese before sprinkling it in the skillet.*

- *When the tuiles have cooled about 5 minutes in Step 3 and are still warm, drape them over the bottom of an overturned shot glass and allow them to finish cooling into the shape of a small bowl.*

Utensils of any material are safe to use with cast iron.

Skillet-Pressed Corn Tortillas

Time: 1 hour 15 minutes
Yield: 16 tortillas

With a skillet, you are never more than two ingredients away from fresh corn tortillas. Use in Chilaquiles (page 25) or serve with Charred Tomato Salsa (page 70).

At Mexican markets, it's often possible to find *masa*, fresh dough for corn tortillas. Much more widely available is *masa harina*, the dry corn flour that can be combined with water to make your own tortilla dough.

Unless you plan on making a lot of tortillas and/or have a remarkable amount of cabinet space, you don't need a tortilla press. And while it's possible to flatten and shape tortillas with a rolling pin, there's a much less fussy method: Use your skillet to flatten them.

INGREDIENTS

2 cups instant corn masa mix (such as Maseca)

1¹/2 cups water

1 Cut a gallon-size zip-top freezer bag in two to yield two thick sheets of plastic.

2 Place the masa mix in a large bowl and slowly add the water while stirring with a fork. After all the water is added, knead the dough until it is smooth, about 3 minutes. The dough should be very soft and not sticky. If it is too dry, add 1 tablespoon water at a time and knead to incorporate. If the dough is too wet, let it rest uncovered for 5 minutes, then knead again. Once the mixture is the right consistency, cover with a damp kitchen towel.

3 Roll 2 tablespoons of the dough (1¹/4 ounces) into a 1¹/2-inch ball, about the size of a golf ball. Place the ball between the plastic sheets on the work surface and flatten it with your palm to produce a disk about 3 inches in diameter. Then use the skillet to press down to produce a disk 5 to 6 inches in diameter.

4 Peel the flattened tortilla from the plastic and place it on a damp kitchen towel with another damp towel on top of it. Repeat Steps 3 and 4 with the remaining dough.

5 Preheat the skillet over medium heat for 2 minutes.

6 Place a tortilla on the skillet and cook until the edges begin to dry and curl up, about 2 minutes. (As the skillet heats up, this may be as little as 1 minute.) Flip the tortilla and cook another 1 to 2 minutes on the other side. When done, both sides should be dry; a few dark spots are okay.

7 Place the finished tortilla on a dry kitchen towel and fold the towel over itself to envelop the tortilla and keep warm for serving. Repeat Steps 6 and 7 with the remaining tortillas. Turn down the heat, if necessary, so the tortillas don't burn before they cook through. If you're not using the tortillas immediately, refrigerate them in a zip-top storage bag.

TIP

- **To reheat the tortillas, place them on a hot skillet and heat each side until just warm, 5 to 10 seconds. Or wrap them in a damp paper towel and microwave them for just a few seconds.**

Fainá
(Chickpea Flatbread)

Time: 1 hour
Yield: Serves 8

Here, the cast iron skillet stands in for the flat pizza pan on which this simple and satisfying dish is usually cooked.

When I lived in Buenos Aires, there was a pizza place about two blocks from my apartment. It did a steady business at all hours of the day and night and, most important, did the critical work of introducing me to *fainá*.

The dish was imported from Italy, where it's known as *farinata*. At my local pizza shop—and at countless others across the city—it was sold in slices and stacked with a piece of pizza, combining for a double-decker swipe at hunger.

Could the skillet reproduce the chickpea flatbread I remembered? As it turns out, yes. Perfectly.

INGREDIENTS

2 cups chickpea flour

1 teaspoon salt

1 cup warm water

¼ cup plus 1 tablespoon extra-virgin olive oil

❶ Preheat the oven to 450°F with the skillet on the middle rack.

❷ In a large bowl, use a wooden spoon to mix the chickpea flour, salt, water, and the ¼ cup olive oil until thoroughly combined. Allow the batter to rest for 30 minutes.

❸ Carefully remove the skillet from the oven, pour in the remaining 1 tablespoon olive oil, and swirl it around to coat the skillet.

Fainá (Chickpea Flatbread), page 61

4 Pour the batter into the skillet and place it in the oven. Bake until the edges are golden brown, about 20 minutes.

5 Remove the skillet from the oven and transfer it to a rack to cool slightly, about 10 minutes. Serve hot. Leftovers can be stored for 1 day at room temperature in the skillet, covered loosely with plastic wrap. Slices can be wrapped in plastic wrap and frozen in a zip-top freezer bag for up to 3 months.

Variation

- *While fainá is traditionally served as an accompaniment to pizza, you can nudge it more in the direction of a main course by almost turning it into a pizza itself: Once the fainá has finished baking, top it with slices of tomato and shredded cheese and broil until the cheese is bubbly, about 5 minutes.*

Spinach and Feta Dip

Time: 30 minutes
Yield: Serves 8

There's nothing like a hot-from-the-oven dip that stays warm from the heat of the skillet.

Making a dip in a skillet is a noble calling, but it's a bit of a balancing act. You want the final product to be dense enough that it stays spreadable, but not so thick that it stays lodged in the skillet. Greek yogurt helps here. It provides a perfectly tangy base for the rest of the ingredients and, since it's had much of its liquid removed, it doesn't release liquid into the dip. The other thing to watch is the spinach, which is naturally full of water. This is why the step of squeezing it dry must not be skipped.

The resulting dip is something that perches beautifully on vegetables, slices of bread, or crackers.

INGREDIENTS

1 (10-ounce) package frozen chopped spinach, thawed and drained

1 (8-ounce) package cream cheese, cut into 16 pieces and softened

2 cups plain 2% Greek yogurt (see Note)

1 cup crumbled feta cheese (about 5 ounces)

1 scallion, both green and white parts, chopped

2 tablespoons chopped, drained, oil-packed sun-dried tomatoes

1/2 teaspoon freshly ground black pepper

Crackers, pita bread, sliced baguette, or carrot and celery sticks, for serving

NOTE

- *Using 2% Greek yogurt provides a good compromise between full-fat and nonfat yogurt, but those may be used to either increase or decrease the richness of the dip.*

1 Preheat the oven to 425°F with one rack in the middle.

2 Use paper towels to absorb the liquid from the spinach.

3 In a medium-size bowl, combine the spinach, cream cheese, yogurt, half the feta cheese, half the scallions, the tomatoes, and the pepper. Scrape the mixture into the skillet and sprinkle with the remaining feta.

4 Bake until the mixture is bubbly around the edges, about 20 minutes. Remove from the oven and garnish with the remaining feta and scallions. Scoop into ramekins to serve very hot, or allow the skillet to cool until no longer too hot to touch, about 15 minutes, and serve the dip from the skillet. Leftovers can be refrigerated in a covered container for up to 2 days.

Variation
• *Add ¼ cup chopped black olives in Step 3.*

TIP
• **Let any leftover dip double as salad dressing. Toss it with a green salad or just cucumbers, thinning the leftover dip with extra-virgin olive oil if desired.**

Pizza Dip

You can make pizza in a skillet, but you can also fast-track things by skipping the crust altogether and spreading this hearty, cheesy dip on a baguette.

Time: 20 minutes
Yield: Serves 4

Making dough is by far the most time-consuming part of making pizza from scratch. So what about a pizza recipe that cuts to the chase? What about something that assumes you have the bread angle covered—whether with a crusty baguette or a stack of pita bread—and lets you focus on the toppings?

The skillet takes care of cooking the sausage and sautéing the vegetables, and then slides right under the broiler to get the cheese nicely browned and bubbly. When it's finished, there's no need to stand on formality and dish out individual servings. Leave the dip in the skillet, if you'd like, and dig in with some pita bread. Or spread it on a baguette that's been halved lengthwise.

INGREDIENTS

8 ounces mild Italian sausage, casings removed

1 small white or yellow onion, diced

1 small clove garlic, minced

8 ounces white mushrooms, sliced

1 (14½-ounce) can diced tomatoes, well drained

1 small green bell pepper, stemmed, seeded, and diced

¼ cup sliced, pitted black olives

1 teaspoon dried oregano

1 teaspoon dried basil

1 cup shredded mozzarella or four-cheese pizza mix

Crusty baguette or pita bread, for serving

1 Preheat the skillet over medium-high heat for 2 minutes. Preheat the broiler.

Pizza Dip, page 67

2 Sauté the sausage, onion, garlic, and mushrooms, breaking up the sausage with a fork as it cooks. Continue to sauté until the sausage is cooked through and the mushrooms are beginning to soften and give off liquid, about 5 minutes.

3 Pour off as much fat and liquid from the skillet as possible. Turn the heat to medium and stir in the tomatoes, pepper, olives, oregano, and basil. Cook until the mixture just begins to bubble and the mushrooms are soft, about 3 minutes.

4 Sprinkle with the cheese and place the skillet under the broiler until the cheese starts to bubble and brown. This could take 5 minutes, but check after 2 minutes, because broiler intensities vary.

5 Remove the skillet from the broiler and transfer it to a rack to cool slightly, about 5 minutes. Serve hot, with bread. Leftovers can be refrigerated in a covered container for up to 2 days.

Variation

- *Substitute spicy Italian sausage for mild, or add a pinch of chili flakes with the sausage in Step 2.*

TIP

- **The vegetables will release some juices while they cook. Drain the tomatoes well and drain as much liquid from the skillet as possible in Step 3 to keep the dip from being too wet.**

Charred Tomato Salsa

Time: 20 minutes
Yield: About 2 cups

When an open fire or barbecue isn't an option, a skillet brings the heat and flavor indoors.

Raw tomatoes, onions, and garlic make a fine salsa, but charring the components first brings the flavors into balance. Fortunately, the skillet is perfect for withstanding the high heat of the broiler. The sweetness of the tomatoes jumps to the fore; the bite of the onions and garlic mellows.

You can't go wrong serving this salsa with tortilla chips, but it also pairs particularly well with grilled chicken or beef.

INGREDIENTS

2 medium-size tomatoes

1 small white or yellow onion, quartered

4 cloves garlic, unpeeled

Salt

¼ cup water

Adobo sauce (from a 7-ounce can of chipotles in adobo)

Tortilla chips, for serving (optional)

NOTE

- *Chipotle peppers are dried, smoked jalapeños. Adobo is the smoky, hot, red sauce that surrounds them in the can. For more heat, use more sauce—or even an entire chipotle pepper. But it's best to start with the relatively modest 1 teaspoon—which gives the salsa a definite kick without setting off the sprinklers—and increase the heat only after tasting.*

1 Preheat the skillet under the broiler for 2 minutes.

2 Place the tomatoes, onion, and garlic in the skillet and broil them until the tomato skins are blistered. This could take 5 minutes, but check after 3 minutes, because broiler intensity varies. Use tongs to flip the vegetables and broil them until the other side of the tomatoes is also blistered, about another 5 minutes.

3 Remove the vegetables from the skillet and allow the tomatoes and garlic to cool until they can be handled safely, about 5 minutes. Remove and discard the skin from the tomatoes and garlic.

4 Place the tomatoes, onion, and garlic in a food processor or blender with ¼ teaspoon salt, the water, and 1 teaspoon adobo sauce, and pulse until smooth.

5 Taste and add more adobo sauce or salt as necessary. Serve with tortilla chips. Leftovers can be refrigerated in a covered container for up to 5 days or frozen in a zip-top freezer bag for 3 months.

Cast iron storage can double as decor.

Roasted Shredded Brussels Sprouts

Time: 1 hour
Yield: Serves 2

The high heat of the skillet and oven transform this vegetable with a sometimes rocky reputation into something appealing, crunchy, and even slightly sweet.

Brussels sprouts get a bad rap. What vegetable wouldn't if it was so often boiled to within an inch of its life? Resurrecting the reputation of the Brussels sprout requires a two-pronged approach: Texture and flavor both play a role. The intense heat of the skillet gives the Brussels sprouts the chance to get browned and crispy in a way that boiling would never afford them. That same heat brings out their natural sweetness, and the transformed vegetable that emerges may have you declaring a Brussels sprouts renaissance.

INGREDIENTS

1 pound Brussels sprouts

¼ cup extra-virgin olive oil or 4 tablespoons Clarified Butter (page 52), melted

¼ teaspoon salt

½ teaspoon freshly ground black pepper

1 Preheat the oven to 450°F with one rack in the middle.

2 Trim the stem end from each Brussels sprout and remove any sad-looking outer leaves. Use a food processor with a shredding disk to coarsely shred the sprouts. Or shred them by hand: Cut each trimmed sprout from stem end to top into

Roasted Shredded Brussels Sprouts, page 73

thin slices, then cut across each slice to yield very thin strips.

3 Toss the shredded sprouts with the olive oil, salt, and pepper. Spread the sprouts in the skillet.

4 Place the skillet in the oven and roast for 15 minutes. Remove the skillet and quickly stir. Return the skillet to the oven and finish roasting until very well browned, about 15 minutes more.

5 Remove the skillet from the oven and serve hot.

Variations

- *In Step 4, add 5 minutes to each cooking time to blacken the Brussels sprouts and get them even crispier.*

- *In Step 5, add 2 tablespoons freshly grated Parmesan cheese just after the Brussels sprouts emerge from the oven. Stir the Brussels sprouts to coat them with the cheese, then add more cheese to taste.*

- *Before Step 1, cook 3 strips bacon over medium-low heat on the stovetop until crisp, about 15 minutes. (The low temperature allows more of the fat to melt out.) Remove the bacon from the skillet and set it aside to cool. Use the bacon fat in the skillet to coat the Brussels sprouts in Step 3 and eliminate the salt. While the Brussels sprouts are in the oven, finely chop the bacon. In Step 5, add the bacon to the sprouts and stir to distribute it evenly before serving.*

Salt-Roasted Potatoes

A white bed of salt offers a striking presentation set against the black of the skillet.

Time: 1 hour
Yield: Serves 2

There is an incredible amount of salt in this dish. But you won't be eating it. Instead, it will be cradling and insulating your potatoes—providing some close-up, intense heat and locking in moisture.

I tried this method cooking shrimp first, but quickly found that unless you use shrimp with the heads on, the tails on, and the shells perfectly intact, salt is bound to seep in. So while it was possible, it was hardly foolproof. Potatoes, however, have their own little jackets—the perfect built-in barrier against the salt. Yes, you can generally eat the skins, too, but they do provide a level of insurance: The salt tends not to stick to them, but even if it does you can still eat the rest of the potato.

Now, here was my concern with the skillet: Would all that salt harm the cast iron? I pictured rusted-out hunks of metal by the seaside, marred by corrosion and time. (My mind wanders, okay?) As a practical matter, you wouldn't want to store your skillet in salt. Or leave it at the bottom of the ocean. But we're talking an hour or so here. Clean out the skillet, as usual, and you'll be fine.

This one is worth serving right from the skillet. Seeing the potatoes emerge from beneath the salt crust is pure theater.

INGREDIENTS

3 pounds (about 6 cups) kosher salt

**1 pound baby potatoes
(1½- to 2-inch diameter)**

**Unsalted butter or extra-virgin olive oil,
for serving**

1 Preheat the oven to 450°F with one rack in the middle.

2 Pour about half the salt in the skillet, nestle the potatoes in it, and then pour the remaining salt over the potatoes, covering them completely.

3 Place the skillet in the oven and roast until a knife can easily pierce a potato, about 50 minutes.

4 Remove the skillet from the oven and transfer it to a rack to cool slightly before serving, about 10 minutes. Serve the potatoes directly from the skillet: To remove the potatoes, use a spoon to crack the salt crust and dig out around each potato. (Some potatoes will probably make this easier by having an air pocket around their sides, but the salt on top must be removed.) With a spoon, lift each potato from its bottom to extract it without breaking the potato skin. With the potato over the skillet, brush off any salt clinging to its skin before transferring it to a plate.

5 Serve warm with butter or olive oil.

Variation

- *Nestle a few sprigs of fresh thyme or a few fresh sage leaves among the potatoes, making sure that they, too, are well covered by the salt to avoid burning.*

TIP

- **Make a note of how many potatoes go into the skillet. You'll thank yourself later when you're poking around the salt trying to remember if you've retrieved them all.**

Bacon-Potato Skillet Bread

Use this to wrap up a simple salad of microgreens and tomatoes and you have a complete one-handed meal.

Time: 1 hour 30 minutes

Yield: 8 skillet breads

Flatbread can sometimes mean something like a pizza—a distinct crust and distinct toppings. But that's not the case here.

This flatbread incorporates the "toppings" into the bread itself, rolled into the dough and revealed in cross section as little layers of bacon and potato goodness throughout.

Cooking the bacon first is doing not just yourself a favor, but your skillet, too. All that bacon fat will continue to season it wonderfully.

INGREDIENTS

8 ounces bacon, coarsely chopped

1 medium-size russet potato (about 8 ounces), unpeeled, cut into 1/2-inch cubes

2 cups unbleached all-purpose flour, plus more for kneading and shaping

1 teaspoon salt

3/4 cup water, plus more if needed

Neutral-flavored oil (such as canola or peanut), for frying

1 Preheat the oven to 400°F with one rack in the middle. Line a large plate with paper towels.

2 While the oven heats, cook the bacon in the skillet over medium-low heat, stirring occasionally, until crisp, about 15 minutes. Transfer the bacon to the plate. Pour off and set aside 2 tablespoons of the bacon fat; leave the rest in the skillet.

3 Place the potato cubes in the skillet, stir to coat them in bacon fat, and place the skillet in the oven. Roast until the potatoes are soft and golden brown, about 20 minutes. While the potatoes are roasting, proceed with the steps below.

Bacon-Potato Skillet Bread, page 79

4 In a large bowl, using a wooden spoon, or in the bowl of a stand mixer fitted with the dough hook, combine the flour and salt. Add the water and the reserved bacon fat and stir or mix on low speed to incorporate. If the dough is too dry and there is still loose flour, add more water 1 tablespoon at a time.

5 If using a mixer, knead on medium speed for 3 minutes. If kneading by hand, dust a work surface lightly with flour, turn out the dough onto it, and knead for about 5 minutes. The dough should be smooth.

6 Break the dough into eight pieces and roll each piece into a 1½-inch ball, about the size of a golf ball. Keep the dough balls covered with plastic wrap or a damp kitchen towel.

7 Again dust the work surface lightly with flour. Flatten a ball with your hand to a 2-inch disk, then use a rolling pin to roll it into a circle 5 inches in diameter. Dust with flour as necessary to prevent sticking. Repeat with the remaining dough, keeping the circles covered once rolled.

8 When the potatoes are cooked, remove them from the oven. Transfer them to the plate with the bacon to drain slightly, then place the potatoes and bacon in a medium-size bowl. Mash them together with a fork until the bacon is well distributed throughout the potatoes.

9 Place 2 tablespoons of the filling in the center of a dough circle. Bring the edges up to surround the filling and pinch them together to contain it. Press down with your hand to flatten the bundle into a disk. Flip the disk over so that the pinched side is down, then use the rolling pin to roll it into a circle 6 inches in diameter, flouring as necessary to prevent sticking.

10 Brush off the excess flour, place the bread on a plate, and cover it with plastic wrap or a damp kitchen towel. Repeat Step 9 with the remaining dough and filling. Brush off excess flour and add each to the plate with the others. The breads can be refrigerated for up to 2 hours before cooking.

11 Preheat the skillet over medium heat for 2 minutes.

12 Add 1 teaspoon oil to the skillet. Place one bread in the skillet. Cook until the bottom of the bread starts to brown in spots, about 3 minutes. Flip the bread and cook for 2 minutes on the other side.

13 Remove the bread from the skillet, transfer it to a clean plate, and cover with foil to keep warm. Repeat with the remaining breads, adding more oil as needed. Serve warm. Leftovers can be refrigerated in a covered container or zip-top storage bag for up to 2 days.

Buttered Basmati Rice

There are those who like the crispy bits at the bottom of the skillet and those I just don't understand.

Time: 1 hour
Yield: Serves 4

Some versions of this recipe would have you cooking the rice in a separate pot, or removing the rice to add some butter to it. Here, it all happens together, in the skillet.

I don't know whether the tendency to gravitate toward the crispy bits of just about any dish is influenced by genetics, but I can confidently say that, one way or another, I followed in my mom's footsteps. I have a propensity for going after that last, delicious crispy bit—whether it's stuck to the spatula, hanging out at the bottom of the pan, or lingering (neglected!) on someone else's plate.

The beauty of this dish is simply this: The crispy bits are celebrated and integral. Rather than leave them lurking in the bottom of the skillet, you can unabashedly get those crispy bits without the slightest hint of reservation or shame.

Which I've heard is a thing for some people.

INGREDIENTS

3 cups plus 2 tablespoons water

1¼ teaspoons salt

1½ cups basmati rice

4 tablespoons (½ stick) unsalted butter

1 Over medium-high heat, bring the 3 cups of water and the salt to a boil in the skillet.

2 While the water is coming to a boil, rinse the rice in a fine sieve until the water runs clear. The water will be cloudy at first.

3 Pour the drained rice into the boiling water and stir to distribute the rice evenly. Turn the heat to medium and continue cooking the rice at a low boil, turning down the heat if it begins to boil too vigorously. Cook until almost all of the water is absorbed and the rice is just shy of fully cooked (it should still have a distinct bite), about 10 minutes.

4 Turn the heat to medium low and use a spatula to pile the rice to one side of the skillet to expose half of the skillet's bottom. Add 1 tablespoon of the butter to the skillet, spread it around so that the surface is covered in butter, replace the rice, and repeat with the other half of the skillet.

5 Smooth the surface of the rice and add the remaining 2 tablespoons water. Dot the rice with the remaining 2 tablespoons butter and place a tight lid on the top of the skillet or cover it tightly with aluminum foil. Cook the rice for 30 minutes, until the water is absorbed and a crust has formed on the bottom of the skillet.

6 Remove the skillet from the heat and transfer it to a rack to stand for 10 minutes.

7 Uncover the skillet and fluff the rice with a fork, leaving the crust at the bottom in place. To serve, spoon out the rice onto a serving platter, then spoon out the crust on top. Leftovers can be refrigerated in a covered container for up to 2 days.

Monkey Pretzel Bread

Tiny balls of dough bake up into the shareable, tearable fun of monkey bread with a pretzel crust.

Time: 1 hour 45 minutes
Cool: 1 hour
Yield: 32 mini rolls

City Bakery in Manhattan is widely credited with inventing the pretzel croissant, a version of which eventually made its way into other stores and bakeries. I finally realized the extent to which pretzelization—the technical term—had taken off when I was standing in a convenience store in Japan and my eyes fell upon a package. To me, the writing on the package was indecipherable. But the pretzel croissant inside was unmistakable.

It's not just croissants—a lot of doughs can be pretzelized. The distinctive brown crust of a pretzel comes from treating the dough with an alkali, usually lye in commercial bakeries. But lye is as dangerous as it is powerful, so baking soda—another alkali—is used here. (See Variations for a tweak to supercharge the baking soda and get an extra pretzel-y exterior.)

One sticking point: That wet alkaline solution sitting in your skillet doesn't do your cast iron any favors. Fortunately, parchment paper can protect it while the bread bakes.

For a final touch, an egg wash is brushed on to give the bread a nice shine.

This pillowy monkey bread emerges from the oven a triumph of food science, taste, and, of course, the skillet.

Monkey Pretzel Bread, page 85

INGREDIENTS

Dough

2¼ cups unbleached all-purpose flour, plus more for kneading

1 teaspoon instant yeast

1 tablespoon sugar

½ teaspoon salt

¾ cup milk (see Note)

1 large egg

1 tablespoon unsalted butter, melted and cooled

Nonstick cooking spray or neutral-flavored oil (such as canola or peanut)

Soaking mixture and topping

½ cup baking soda

4 cups hot tap water

1 large egg, beaten with 2 teaspoons water

2 tablespoons freshly grated Parmesan cheese

NOTE

- *Use whole milk if available. It adds richness to the dough.*

1 Make the dough: In a large bowl, using a wooden spoon, or in the bowl of a stand mixer fitted with the dough hook, combine the flour, yeast, sugar, and salt.

2 Measure the milk in a measuring cup, then use a fork to whisk in the egg and butter. Add this to the flour mixture and stir to incorporate or mix on low speed.

3 If using a mixer, knead on medium speed for about 5 minutes, until the dough releases from the sides of the bowl. If kneading by hand, lightly dust a work surface with flour, turn the dough out onto it, and knead for 6 to 8 minutes, until the dough is smooth and soft.

4 Spray a large bowl with cooking spray or wipe it with a thin coat of oil. Shape the dough into a ball and place in the bowl. Cover it tightly with a lid or plastic wrap and let rise at room temperature until puffy, about 1 hour 30 minutes.

5 Preheat the oven to 375°F with one rack in the middle.

6 Turn out the dough onto a work surface and punch it down to deflate it. Push straight down with a large sharp knife (do not use a sawing motion) to divide the dough into four equal parts. Divide each part into four equal parts again to yield 16 pieces total. Divide those pieces in half to yield 32 pieces. Form each piece into a ball about 1 inch in diameter by bringing together two ends, then gathering more dough near those two ends until a rough sphere is created with a pinched seam on the bottom and a taut, rounded surface on the top.

7 Line the skillet with parchment paper. Any excess will serve as handles later to lift out the bread once it has baked.

8 Soak and top the bread: In a medium-size bowl, stir the baking soda into the hot tap water. Place the dough balls in the baking soda solution and let them soak for 2 minutes, stirring occasionally. Use a slotted spoon to lift the dough balls from the baking soda solution, allow them to drain over the bowl, then arrange them seam side down in the parchment. If the dough balls have unraveled slightly, just pinch them back together at the bottom and be sure to place them seam side down. Most dough pieces will touch when the skillet is full, but it's okay if there are a few gaps.

9 Brush the dough balls with the egg wash, then sprinkle them with the Parmesan. Bake until the top is a rich golden brown, 25 to 30 minutes.

10 Remove the skillet from the oven and lift out the bread with the parchment paper attached. Transfer the bread to a rack to cool for 10 minutes before peeling off the parchment paper and returning the bread to the rack to cool completely, about 1 hour. Leftover bread can be broken into single-serving pieces and frozen in a zip-top freezer bag.

Variations

- *Substitute coarse sea salt or poppy seeds for the Parmesan—or add one along with another.*

- *Add ½ cup shredded cheese such as sharp Cheddar toward the end of kneading in Step 3.*

- *To supercharge your baking soda and make it more alkaline—and thus the bread even more pretzel-like—take a page from food science writer Harold McGee and bake the baking soda. The resulting powder builds a darker crust but, unlike lye, doesn't require goggles and rubber gloves to handle. (Though do avoid handling it, and wash your hands if you come in contact with it.) Here's how to do it: Preheat the oven to 300°F with one rack in the middle. Line the skillet with aluminum foil and spread the baking soda on the foil. Bake 1 hour. The baked baking soda can be stored at room temperature indefinitely in a clearly marked, nonreactive container; glass is a good choice. When you're ready to shape the bread, use the baked baking soda in Step 8 and pour 4 cups room-temperature water into a second medium-size bowl. Follow the directions for shaping and soaking, then dunk the dough briefly in the plain water after the 2-minute soak before arranging the dough in the skillet.*

CHAPTER 4

Main Courses

Pressed Grilled Cheese

Time: 10 minutes
Yield: Serves 1

Marry those layers of bread and cheese by weighing down the sandwich with a skillet (or other cookware) for a crispier outside and a gooier inside.

There's an unlikely ingredient in this grilled cheese: mayonnaise. That mayo provides the foundation for another level of cheese in this sandwich: the Parmesan crust grilled onto the outside. Not only does mayo help the Parmesan adhere to the sandwich, it makes sure the sandwich develops a nice crunchy exterior when it meets the heat of the skillet.

To bring the sandwich together, place another skillet if you have one—or a heavy pot or pan if you don't—on top of the assembled sandwich in the skillet to press down on the sandwich.

INGREDIENTS

2 tablespoons mayonnaise

1 tablespoon freshly grated Parmesan cheese

2 thick (about ¾ inch) slices sandwich bread

3 ounces Cheddar cheese, thinly sliced or shredded

NOTE

- *If your bread is thinner, reduce the cheese to 2 ounces to maintain the bread-to-cheese ratio, and use a lighter pot to weigh down the sandwich while it cooks.*

1 Preheat the skillet over medium heat for 2 minutes.

2 While the skillet preheats, combine the mayonnaise and Parmesan. Spread half on one side of each slice of bread.

3 Place a slice of bread, mayonnaise side down, on the skillet. Distribute the Cheddar evenly on the bread. Top with the second slice of bread, mayonnaise side up.

4 Lay a piece of aluminum foil on top of the sandwich and place a pot or another skillet on top of the foil to press the sandwich.

5 Cook the first side until the bread is golden brown and the cheese has started to melt, about 2 minutes. (Remove the weight and foil to check.) Use a spatula to flip the sandwich. Replace the foil and weight, and continue to cook until the second side is golden brown and the cheese has completely melted, about 2 minutes.

6 Remove the sandwich from the skillet. Slice into halves or quarters, and serve hot.

Variations

- *Instead of Cheddar cheese, try Taleggio, Gruyère, Gouda, Swiss, Havarti, or American.*

- *For a twist, try adding one of the following in Step 3 before the second slice of bread: tomato slices, thinly sliced apple or pear, sliced fresh figs, preserves, sliced deli meat, cooked bacon, Dijon mustard, or sriracha.*

Grilled Vegetable and Cheddar Nachos

Time: 45 minutes

Yield: Serves 4

Take back this dish from the grip of cheese goo and mystery meat toppings! Skillet-grilled vegetables team up with more lightly cooked vegetables to make this a respectable meal.

This isn't exactly a green salad—there are plenty of chips and cheese to go around—but it's a step up in the world for what can sometimes best be described as a guilty pleasure.

Of course, guilt and pleasure are in the eye of the beholder. Adjust the ratio of cheese, chips, and veggies as you see fit, keeping in mind that anything more than 8 ounces of tortilla chips will be a tight fit in a 10-inch skillet.

One important note before diving in: Broilers vary in intensity. Keep an eye on the vegetables as they broil. There's a fine line between beautifully blackened and tragically burned. Mealtime works better if you stay on the right side of the line.

INGREDIENTS

2 tablespoons extra-virgin olive oil

1/4 teaspoon ground cumin

1 large green bell pepper, cut in half, stemmed, and seeded

1 large red bell pepper, cut in half, stemmed, and seeded

2 medium-size plum tomatoes

1 small white or yellow onion, quartered

1 small zucchini, split lengthwise

8 ounces tortilla chips (see Note)

1 1/2 cups shredded Cheddar cheese

Sour cream or Mexican crema, pickled jalapeños, sliced avocado, and salsa or hot sauce, for serving

- *Thick tortilla chips work best at standing up to the weight of the other ingredients. Reduced-sodium chips are a good option if available (the cheese and salsa will provide enough salt).*

1 Preheat the skillet under the broiler for 2 minutes.

2 In a large bowl, combine the olive oil and cumin. Toss one half of the green pepper, one half of the red pepper, one whole tomato, the onion, and the zucchini with the oil and arrange the vegetables on the preheated skillet. Pour any oil left in the bowl over the vegetables.

3 Place the skillet under the broiler and cook until the tomato and peppers are blistered. This could take about 5 minutes or even longer, but check after 3 minutes, because broiler intensity varies. Use tongs to flip the vegetables and broil until the tomato and peppers are again blistered and blackened in spots, about another 5 minutes. Zucchini may not blacken but should be soft. Do not hesitate to broil the vegetables another 5 minutes if necessary to achieve the blistered and blackened spots.

4 Remove the vegetables from the skillet and allow them to cool until they can be handled, about 5 minutes.

5 Preheat the oven to 450°F with one rack in the middle.

6 Chop the cooked vegetables into bite-size pieces and blot them with a paper towel or clean kitchen towel to remove some of the moisture. Chop the raw vegetables into bite-size pieces and add to the cooked vegetables.

7 Spread half of the chips in the skillet in an even layer. Sprinkle half of the cheese and half of the vegetables over the chips. Repeat with the remaining chips, vegetables, and cheese, ending with the cheese.

8 Bake until the cheese is melted and bubbly, about 15 minutes.

9 Remove the skillet from the oven. Serve hot, with sour cream, pickled jalapeños, avocado, and salsa or hot sauce.

Grilled Vegetable and Cheddar Nachos, page 93

Peanut and Tofu Skillet Stir-Fry

Time: 15 minutes
Yield: Serves 2

The wok is the traditional stir-fry vessel, but your skillet can do it, too!

I n this stir-fry, the bulk of the cooking time is spent crisping the tofu. But if you're in a hurry, feel free to go with less-crispy tofu and shave off some minutes.

It's important that the tofu not be too crowded in the skillet—each piece needs direct contact with the high heat of the skillet to crisp up well. Trial and error showed that 1 pound of tofu is the most a 10-inch skillet can handle.

Once the tofu has crisped on a few sides, the skillet can handle a bit more volume—or you can start trading out elements to get different flavors (see Variations).

INGREDIENTS

2 tablespoons soy sauce

2 tablespoons fish sauce (see Notes)

2 tablespoons sugar

2 tablespoons lime juice

1/4 teaspoon chili flakes

1/2 pound firm tofu, cut into 1/2-inch cubes (see Note)

3 heads baby bok choi (about 5 ounces), chopped into 1-inch pieces

2 tablespoons neutral-flavored oil (such as canola or peanut)

3 scallions, green and white parts finely chopped

1/4 cup roasted salted peanuts

Cooked rice or rice noodles, for serving (optional)

NOTES

- *Fish sauce adds depth of flavor and umami—that savory fifth taste alongside sour, sweet, bitter, and salty—without being overtly fishy in the finished dish. It's good to have on hand and when refrigerated, lasts practically forever. If you don't have any, substitute an equal amount of Worcestershire sauce for those same briny notes.*

- *Look for tofu packaged in a container with liquid and sold in a refrigerated case. Tofu in shelf-stable packaging won't get as crispy in the skillet.*

1 In a small bowl, combine the soy sauce, fish sauce, sugar, lime juice, and chili flakes.

2 Preheat the skillet over medium-high heat for 2 minutes.

3 While the skillet preheats, use your hands to press the tofu cubes between paper towels to remove moisture.

4 Add the oil to the skillet and wait 30 seconds for it to get hot before carefully adding the tofu.

5 Let the tofu cook undisturbed until golden brown on one side, about 2 minutes. Use a spatula to flip the tofu pieces. Cook until they are golden brown on another side, about 2 minutes.

6 Turn the heat to medium low, add the bok choi and scallions, and flip the tofu again to brown on another side. Cook until the scallions are just softened and the bok choi greens are slightly wilted, about 2 minutes.

7 Remove the skillet from the heat and add the sauce and peanuts. Use a spatula to stir until just heated through, about 30 seconds.

8 Serve hot, on its own or accompanied by rice or rice noodles, pouring the sauce from the skillet over the top.

Variations

- *Add up to 1 cup cooked leftover vegetables with the scallions and bok choi in Step 6.*

- *Replace half the bok choi with other chopped hearty vegetables such as carrot or broccoli.*

- *Substitute 2 tablespoons toasted sesame seeds for the peanuts.*

TIP

- **Make the sauce ahead of time and the meal comes together even more quickly. It can be refrigerated in a covered glass container for up to 1 week. Stir or shake just before using.**

Potato-Crusted Ham Quiche

Time: 1 hour 30 minutes

Yield: Serves 6

The direct heat of the skillet crisps the shredded potatoes while the quiche sets.

A quiche traditionally has a crust, sure, but no one said what that crust had to be made of—or if they did, I wasn't listening.

So what about a crust made of potato? Would that work? As it turns out, yes. The potato underneath absorbs the flavors of the eggs, ham, and vegetables, while the crust lining the skillet rim above the quiche stays crispy and crunchy. (This is why it's important to pile the crust high along the edge of the skillet—no missing out on crunchy bits!)

INGREDIENTS

3 tablespoons olive oil

1¼ cups diced white or yellow onion (about 1 medium-size onion)

8 ounces white mushrooms, sliced

1 teaspoon salt

5 ounces baby spinach

½ cup diced cooked ham

2 medium-size russet potatoes (about 1 pound total)

½ teaspoon freshly ground black pepper

6 large eggs

½ cup milk

½ teaspoon Dijon mustard

1 cup shredded mild cheese (such as Fontina, Gruyère, or Swiss)

1 Preheat the oven to 450°F with one rack in the middle.

2 Add 2 teaspoons of the oil to the skillet and heat over medium heat until the oil is hot, about 2 minutes. Add the onion, mushrooms, and ¼ teaspoon of salt. Cook, stirring occasionally, until the onions are softened and the mushrooms are cooked through, about 10 minutes.

3 Add the spinach in two batches, cooking and stirring each time until the spinach wilts, about 30 seconds. The spinach will barely fit in the skillet at first, but will cook down quickly when stirred. Remove the skillet from the heat.

4 Drain off as much liquid as possible and scrape the vegetables into a large bowl. Add the ham and set aside. Wipe the skillet clean.

5 Use a paper towel to rub 1 teaspoon of the oil into the skillet.

6 Using the coarse side of a box grater or a food processor, shred the potatoes. (You should have about 3½ cups.) Squeeze the shreds in a clean kitchen towel until they're as dry as you can manage. (The potato might discolor the towel. Remove the discoloration by immediately rinsing the towel under cold running water.)

7 In a medium-size bowl, toss the potatoes with the remaining 2 tablespoons oil, ½ teaspoon of the salt, and ¼ teaspoon of the pepper. Press the potatoes into the skillet in an even layer across the bottom and all the way up the sides.

8 Bake until the potatoes are golden brown at the edges, about 30 minutes.

9 Remove the skillet from the oven and set the oven temperature to 325°F.

10 In a medium-size bowl, whisk together the eggs, milk, mustard, and the remaining ¼ teaspoon each of salt and pepper.

11 The ham and vegetables may have given off liquid as they sat. If so, drain it off. Distribute the cheese evenly atop the potato. Spread the ham and vegetables in an even layer over the cheese. Pour in the egg mixture.

12 Bake until the eggs are set at the edges (the center may still jiggle a bit), about 30 minutes. An instant-read thermometer should read 170°F in the center.

13 Remove the skillet from the oven and transfer it to a rack to cool slightly, about 10 minutes. Serve warm or at room temperature. Leftovers can be refrigerated in a covered container for up to 2 days.

Variation

- *Add up to 1 cup chopped bell peppers, chopped broccoli, or halved cherry tomatoes in Step 2.*

TIP

- **The vegetables and ham can be prepared ahead of time. Keep refrigerated in a covered container for up to 2 days. Then pick up again at Step 5, and add about 5 minutes to the baking time to account for the colder ingredients.**

Potato-Crusted Ham Quiche, page 99

Mozzarella and Mushroom Calzone

Time: 45 minutes
Yield: Serves 2

Pizza sometimes gets all the attention, but these pockets of dough and filling more than hold their own.

Inevitably, some of the calzone filling will start to bubble and melt out of its pocket. In fact, that's one of the ways to know they're ready to pull from the oven. One of the advantages of making these in the skillet is that the melted filling won't go too far. So, yes, you can make these on a cookie sheet or a pizza pan, but the skillet keeps things a bit more tidy. Another bonus: The high heat from the skillet on the bottom of the calzone keeps the crust crunchy and golden brown in the face of any moisture from the filling.

INGREDIENTS

Unbleached all-purpose flour, for dusting and rolling

12 ounces pizza dough (store-bought, or see Note and use modified Deep-Dish Pizza recipe)

1 medium-size plum tomato, diced

2 cups shredded mozzarella

1 cup sliced white mushrooms

1/2 teaspoon dried oregano

Olive oil, for brushing the dough

Marinara sauce and freshly grated Parmesan cheese, for serving

NOTE:

• *If using the Deep-Dish Pizza dough on page 108, make the following changes to the ingredients and follow the instructions through Step 3. Use 1 1/4 cups flour, 1 teaspoon sugar, 1/4 teaspoon salt, 3/4 teaspoon instant yeast, and 1/2 cup water. (Omit the cornmeal and olive oil.) The dough will be stiff and not as supple as the original recipe.*

1 Preheat the oven to 400°F with one rack in the middle.

2 Lightly dust a work surface with flour. Divide the dough into two portions.

3 Roll one portion into a ball, flatten it with your palm, then use a rolling pin lightly dusted with flour to roll it into a circle 9 inches in diameter. If the dough starts to resist and snaps back to shape, let it rest a few minutes before continuing.

4 Use a dull knife to gently score a line across the middle of the dough. Do not cut through. Starting about 1/2 inch from the edge and stopping at the line in the center, spread half of the tomato, cheese, mushrooms, and oregano on the dough.

5 Fold the dough at the line, covering the filling. The filling will be piled high; don't be afraid to gently stretch the dough to encompass it. Fold the edge back on itself slightly and use a fork to crimp and seal the edge as you work your way around the dough. Carefully move the calzone into the skillet. Brush the top with olive oil. Use a sharp knife to cut three 1-inch ventilation slits equally spaced across the top of the calzone.

6 Repeat Steps 3 through 5 with the remaining dough and fillings.

7 Place the skillet in the oven and bake until the crusts are golden brown and the fillings are hot and bubbly, about 30 minutes.

8 Remove the skillet from the oven, transfer it to a rack, and let the calzones cool about 5 minutes before serving.

9 Cut each calzone in half and serve with marinara sauce and Parmesan. Serve hot.

Variations

- *Just about anything that works as a pizza topping can work as a calzone filling, with two important considerations:*

  * *Keep the total volume of filling about the same as in this recipe (just over 1 1/2 cups per calzone)—there's not enough room for much more!*

  * *Make sure the filling is not too moist. Before adding any ingredients that are wet or likely to give off water, drain or press them.*

* *Think beyond pizza flavors, too: Use the dough as a blank canvas and the filling as a showcase for stir-fry leftovers, Thanksgiving leftovers (mashed potato and turkey calzones with gravy dipping sauce, anyone?), or those odd bits in the refrigerator.*

- Turn any extra dough into dinner rolls. Two ounces of dough make one dinner roll. Form a piece of dough into a ball about 1 inch in diameter by bringing together two ends, then gathering more dough near those two ends until a rough sphere is created with a pinched seam on the bottom and a taut, rounded surface on the top. Place the dough on the skillet, brush it with melted butter or olive oil, and allow it to rise while the oven preheats to 400°F. Bake until golden brown, about 20 minutes. Baked dinner rolls can be frozen in a zip-top freezer bag and reheated in the oven or allowed to thaw at room temperature.

Mac and Cheese

The pasta and sauce come together right in the skillet.

Time: 30 minutes
Yield: Serves 2

I am no stranger to mac and cheese from a box. And I'm no stranger to recipes that take an hour in the oven. But there is certainly a place for something you make from scratch but is ready in less than 30 minutes on the stovetop.

So many recipes would have you boil the macaroni in one pot and make the sauce in another. But why not cook the macaroni right in the skillet in the first place?

INGREDIENTS

1/2 teaspoon salt

2 cups elbow macaroni

2 tablespoons unsalted butter

3/4 cup evaporated milk

1/2 teaspoon Dijon mustard

Pinch of cayenne pepper

1 1/2 cups shredded sharp Cheddar cheese

1 Fill the skillet two-thirds full of water, add the salt, and bring to a boil over medium-high heat.

2 Add the macaroni, turn the heat to medium, and cook, stirring occasionally, until just shy of al dente. This should take about 10 minutes, but check the pasta package for recommended cooking times and aim for the lower end if a range is given. (The macaroni will continue to cook a bit in the sauce.) When the macaroni is ready, biting into a piece should reveal a very thin core of uncooked pasta.

3 Drain the macaroni and return it to the skillet. Turn the heat to low. Add the butter and stir until it melts.

4 Add the evaporated milk, mustard, and cayenne and stir well to combine. Add the cheese in three batches, stirring frequently as each batch is added and waiting until the cheese has melted before adding the next batch. After about 5 minutes total, the sauce will be smooth and noticeably thicker.

5 Serve hot. Leftovers can be refrigerated in a covered container for up to 2 days.

Deep-Dish Pizza

Thin crust has its place, but sometimes nothing beats the heft of a thick, skillet-size pie.

Time: 2 hours 45 minutes
Cool: 15 minutes
Yield: Serves 6

I lived for more than a decade in Chicago and have definite opinions about deep-dish pizza, though I would never reveal where my pizzeria allegiance lies.

With this recipe, I looked to bring out the best of what Chicago deep-dish can be: in the crust, the slight crunch of the cornmeal; in the sauce, the interplay between sweetness and a mild tang; and in the cheese, straightforward mozzarella accented with a little Parmesan.

Typically, deep-dish pizza is made in, well, a deep pizza pan. But it's a small jump from there to the skillet. Baking the crust about 10 minutes first sets it and helps it stand up to the toppings.

INGREDIENTS

Crust

1¾ cups unbleached all-purpose flour, plus more for dusting and rolling

¼ cup finely ground cornmeal

1 tablespoon sugar

½ teaspoon salt

1 teaspoon instant yeast

Nonstick cooking spray

¾ cup water, at room temperature

2 tablespoons olive oil, plus more for greasing the skillet

Sauce

1 (28-ounce) can no-salt-added crushed tomatoes

¼ teaspoon freshly ground black pepper

1 teaspoon dried oregano

1 small clove garlic, minced

1 tablespoon balsamic vinegar

½ teaspoon salt

Filling

2½ cups shredded mozzarella

½ cup freshly grated Parmesan cheese

- *The sodium content in canned tomatoes can vary widely. Buying no-salt-added tomatoes and adding the salt yourself by taste is a better way to properly season the sauce.*

1 Make the crust: In a large bowl, using a wooden spoon, or in the bowl of a stand mixer fitted with the dough hook, stir the flour, cornmeal, sugar, salt, and yeast until well combined. Add the water and olive oil and mix until no loose flour remains. If the mixture is too dry, add 1 tablespoon water at a time. Allow the dough to stand 15 minutes.

2 If using a mixer, knead on low speed for 5 minutes. If kneading by hand, dust a work surface lightly with flour, turn out the dough onto it, and knead about 7 minutes. The dough should be smooth and very slightly tacky but not sticky.

3 Spray a large bowl with cooking spray or wipe it with a thin coat of oil. Shape the dough into a ball and place in the bowl. Cover tightly with a lid or plastic wrap and allow to rise at room temperature until doubled in size, about 1 hour.

4 Preheat the oven to 400°F with one rack in the middle.

5 Dust a work surface lightly with flour. Turn out the dough onto it and punch it down to deflate it. Cover with plastic wrap and allow it to rest 10 minutes.

6 While the dough rests, make the sauce: Place a fine sieve over a medium-size bowl and pour in the tomatoes. Allow the tomatoes to drain for 5 minutes. Discard the liquid in the bowl (there should be about 1/2 cup liquid). Pour the tomatoes into the bowl and mix in the pepper, oregano, garlic, balsamic vinegar, and salt. Set aside.

7 Coat the bottom and sides of the skillet with a generous layer of olive oil.

8 Use a rolling pin to roll the dough into a circle 13 inches in diameter. If the dough resists stretching, let it rest about 5 minutes before proceeding.

9 Lay the dough in the skillet, pressing down the bottom, sides, and along the top rim. Let the dough rest 10 minutes. Poke the surface, including the sides, with a fork at about 1-inch intervals and make sure the dough is tucked well into where the sides meet the bottom of the skillet.

10 Place the skillet in the oven for 10 minutes to partially bake the crust.

11 Remove the skillet from the oven. Spread the mozzarella across the crust, then top with the sauce. Sprinkle the Parmesan across the top.

12 Place the skillet back in the oven and bake until the crust edges are browned and the cheese is golden, about 30 minutes.

13 Remove the skillet from the oven and transfer to a rack. Allow the pizza to cool until the sauce is no longer runny, at least 15 minutes, before serving warm. Leftovers can be refrigerated in a covered container for up to 2 days.

Variation

- *Add up to 2 cups chopped vegetables, such as onion, bell pepper, mushrooms, or broccoli. Lightly sauté the vegetables in olive oil with a pinch of freshly ground black pepper and salt and drain them of any liquid before adding them after the sauce in Step 11.*

TIPS

- **The sauce can be made up to 5 days ahead and refrigerated in a covered container.**
- **The dough can be made 1 day ahead through Step 2, placed in an oiled bowl, covered, and allowed to rise in the refrigerator. Allow it to come to room temperature and be sure it has doubled in size before continuing with Step 4.**

Tortilla Española

Time: 30 minutes
Cool: 30 minutes
Yield: 8 wedges

Starting this Spanish potato omelet on the stovetop and finishing it under the broiler means cooking it through with no flipping or fussing.

For me, *tortilla española* will always conjure up images of thick slabs of egg and potato crammed indelicately between long halves of baguette and handed out through a window to a long line of hungry students. I was once one of those students.

The window was in a small, dismal shopping center across from one of my classes when I studied in Seville, Spain. Getting so much food for a couple of bucks was a godsend. I didn't dwell too much on whether the food was any good. But you know what? It was. Sometimes simple is best.

Traditionally, the tortilla is cooked on one side, flipped out onto a plate, and then slid back in the pan to finish on the other side. But that's a lot of acrobatics with a hot skillet and partially cooked egg. So this version finishes neatly under the broiler.

Serve the tortilla warm with bread and a salad for dinner, room temperature on toothpicks as finger food, or cold between slices of baguette for a sandwich the next day.

INGREDIENTS

¾ cup olive oil (see Note)

4 medium-size russet potatoes (about 2 pounds total), peeled, cut in half lengthwise, and sliced about ¼-inch thick

1 medium-size white or yellow onion, cut in half and sliced ¼-inch thick

1 teaspoon salt

½ teaspoon freshly ground black pepper

6 large eggs

½ teaspoon baking powder

- *Yes, all of this oil is necessary to cook the potatoes, but if you find that much oil off-putting, fear not. Very little of the oil is absorbed into the potatoes.*

1 Heat the oil in the skillet over medium heat for 2 minutes.

2 Add the potatoes and onions. Sprinkle with ¾ teaspoon of the salt and all the pepper. Cook, stirring occasionally, until the potatoes are soft, about 15 minutes. Turn down the heat if the potatoes or onions begin to brown.

3 In a large bowl, whisk together the eggs, baking powder, and the remaining ¼ teaspoon salt. Use a slotted spoon to transfer the potatoes and onions to the bowl with the eggs, leaving the oil behind in the skillet.

4 Carefully pour off and discard all but about 1 tablespoon of the oil from the skillet. Preheat the broiler. Use the lowest setting if adjustable.

5 Place the skillet over medium-low heat and spread the egg-and-potato mixture evenly in it. Cook until the edges are set and only just beginning to brown, about 5 minutes. (Use a spatula to pull back the edge and check.)

6 Place the skillet under the broiler and broil until the top is set, about 3 minutes.

7 Remove the skillet from the broiler and transfer it to a rack to cool until the tortilla is just warm, about 30 minutes. Slice into wedges and serve. Leftovers can be refrigerated in a covered container for up to 2 days.

TIP

- **Don't throw away those potato skins! Throw them in a quart-size zip-top bag and store them in the freezer. When you've accumulated a full bag, roast them to crispy perfection: Toss them with 1 tablespoon olive oil or bacon fat and ½ teaspoon salt. Place them in a skillet and bake in a preheated 400°F oven until crispy, about 20 minutes, stirring halfway through.**

Pasta with Cherry Tomatoes and Ricotta

Time: 20 minutes
Yield: Serves 2

First char the skins of the tomatoes in the skillet, then bring together the rest of the dish without another pot or pan.

At the end of a long day, the notion of making everything in one pot—namely, one skillet—can be irresistible.

Rather than cooking in a separate pan, the pasta here cooks in the same skillet where the sauce takes shape, absorbing water and some of the tomato juices as it bubbles away. The creaminess of the ricotta makes the finished pasta rich without being overwhelming.

The trick was finding just the right amount of water to use. Too much and the sauce is soupy, too little and the pasta doesn't cook. When the pasta is cooked al dente in this recipe, any remaining liquid in the skillet—imbued with tomato and starch from the pasta—thickens and becomes part of the sauce when the ricotta is stirred in.

INGREDIENTS

30 grape tomatoes or 20 cherry tomatoes (about 12 ounces), cut in half

2½ cups cut fusilli

2 cloves garlic, thinly sliced

Pinch of chili flakes

1 tablespoon extra-virgin olive oil

1 teaspoon salt

¼ teaspoon freshly ground black pepper

2 cups water

½ cup ricotta

Torn fresh basil leaves and freshly grated Parmesan cheese, for garnish

Pasta with Cherry Tomatoes and Ricotta, page 115

1   Preheat the skillet over high heat for 2 minutes.

2   Place the tomatoes in the skillet and cook until the skins are blistered, about 2 minutes.

3   Add the fusilli, garlic, chili flakes, olive oil, salt, and pepper. Carefully add the water and bring to a boil. Turn down the heat if necessary to avoid bubbling over while maintaining a boil. Use a spatula to stir the mixture every few minutes and cook until the pasta is al dente and very little liquid remains, about 10 minutes.

4   Remove the skillet from the heat and stir in the ricotta. Serve hot, garnished with the basil and Parmesan. Leftovers can be refrigerated in a covered container for up to 2 days.

Variation

- *Trade out penne, rotini, or farfalle for the fusilli.*

Ricotta, Spinach, and Mushroom Lasagna

Time: 1 hour 15 minutes

Yield: Serves 4

First sauté the vegetables and make the sauce in the skillet, then layer all of the ingredients to bake in the oven.

Until they make lasagna noodles shaped for the skillet—hey, that day could come!—making lasagna in the skillet is a bit of a "square peg in a round hole" situation. But you can solve this by making the lasagna noodles bend to your will—well, *break* to your will is more like it. The bottom line is that no one will be checking to see if your lasagna noodles are perfectly arranged. As long as you fit them into the skillet, you're good.

Many recipes call for frozen spinach to be drained, but in this case the liquid from the spinach is all part of the plan. It helps to hydrate and cook the noodles.

INGREDIENTS

1 tablespoon olive oil, plus more for greasing the skillet

8 ounces white mushrooms, sliced

1 clove garlic, cut in half and crushed

1 teaspoon fresh thyme leaves, chopped, or 1/4 teaspoon dried thyme

Salt and freshly ground black pepper

1 (10-ounce) package frozen chopped spinach, thawed

1 cup ricotta

1 large egg

3 cups marinara sauce (Store-bought, or Deep-Dish Pizza Sauce, page 108)

4 ounces no-boil lasagna noodles

2 tablespoons freshly grated Parmesan cheese

NOTES

- *If using the Deep-Dish Pizza sauce on page 108, omit the balsamic vinegar and do not drain the tomatoes, but follow the remaining instructions in Step 6.*

- *Depending on the size and shape of your noodles, you may end up with a few extra. The important things: Be willing to break some noodles to fit into any odd-shaped spaces, and don't overlap them or they may not cook fully.*

1 Preheat the oven to 350°F with one rack in the middle. Preheat the skillet over medium heat for 2 minutes.

2 Add the olive oil to the skillet, allow it to heat 1 minute, then add the mushrooms, garlic, thyme, 1/4 teaspoon salt, and 1/4 teaspoon pepper. Cook, stirring occasionally, until the mushrooms

TIP:

- **Pull fresh thyme leaves off their stems by running your fingers from the top down over a cutting board. Check for any twigs before chopping finely.**

soften, about 10 minutes. Taste to check for seasoning and add salt and pepper as necessary. Remove and discard the garlic. Pour the mushrooms and any liquid into a bowl and set aside.

3 In a medium-size bowl, combine the spinach with the ricotta, egg, 1/4 teaspoon salt, and 1/4 teaspoon pepper.

4 Rub a coating of olive oil on the skillet and then layer the ingredients in this order:

- 3/4 cup of the ricotta mixture
- 1 cup of the marinara sauce
- half of the mushrooms and their liquid
- half of the noodles (break the noodles if necessary to cover the whole skillet)
- 3/4 cup of the ricotta mixture
- 1 cup of the marinara sauce
- the remaining mushrooms and any liquid
- the remaining noodles
- the remaining ricotta mixture
- the remaining marinara sauce

5 Sprinkle the Parmesan evenly across the top of the lasagna. Cover the skillet tightly with aluminum foil and place in the oven.

6 Bake until the mixture is bubbling and the lasagna noodles are tender, about 45 minutes.

7 Remove the skillet from the oven and transfer it to a rack to cool slightly, about 10 minutes, before serving hot. Leftovers can be refrigerated in a covered container for up to 2 days.

TIPS

- **The layers of sauce will be quite thin on their own, but don't worry! They will add up to a full skillet of lasagna.**
- **Your noodle placement doesn't have to be picture perfect, but take care not to overlap them. And make sure none are poking up above the sauce.**

The durability of cast iron is just one of its charms.

Single-Skillet Carnitas

Time: 3 hours 30 minutes

Yield: Serves 4

The skillet does double duty here, holding the pork while it simmers gently in liquid and then allowing you to finish the meat with a quick fry at the end.

There are a few things to understand at the outset: First, for the purposes of pig anatomy at the butcher, the butt and the shoulder are the same thing. (This is of course not literally true in the field, where the result would be some very funny-looking pigs.) The point is, you may find the meat for carnitas labeled either pork butt or pork shoulder.

Second, that familiar pulled pork slathered with barbecue sauce and the crispy carnitas perched on a small corn tortilla? Same thing. Well, at the outset anyway.

There is often quite a bit of fat throughout this cut. Don't trim too much of it. You won't end up eating all of it (unless you want to), and it has a job to do: Much of it melts into the bottom of the skillet and provides fat for the meat's final fry.

INGREDIENTS

2 pounds boneless pork shoulder, cut into 2-inch cubes

1 medium-size white or yellow onion, quartered

Salt and freshly ground black pepper

1/2 teaspoon ground cumin

Juice of 1 orange

Juice of 1 lime, plus more if needed

2 cups water, plus more if needed

Corn tortillas (page 59 or store-bought), guacamole, and pico de gallo or salsa (page 70 or store-bought), for serving

NOTE:
- *The salt, pepper, and ground cumin can be replaced by 2 teaspoons Toasted Cumin Seasoning Mix (page 48).*

1. Place the pork and onion in the skillet and sprinkle the meat with 1 teaspoon salt, 1/2 teaspoon pepper, and the cumin. Add the orange and lime juices, then pour in water until the meat is just covered. If a few pieces poke out, it's okay; the meat will break down as it cooks.

2. Place the skillet over medium heat and cook until the water is just simmering, about 10 minutes. If any foam develops on the surface, skim it off with a spoon and discard it.

3. Continue to simmer. Flip the pork every 20 to 30 minutes, and turn the heat to medium low if necessary to maintain a gentle simmer. Cook until the meat is tender and just about falls apart when prodded with a fork, 2 hours to 2 hours 30 minutes.

4. Remove the onion pieces from the skillet and discard them. Turn up the heat to medium high. Cook until the water has largely evaporated and mostly liquid fat remains in the bottom of the skillet, about 10 minutes. (The sound will change from the gurgling of boiling water to the snapping sound of hot fat.)

5. Turn the heat to low. Cook the pork pieces in the fat, flipping them occasionally, until they are well browned, about 15 minutes. Don't overdo it; stop if it appears the pork is becoming too dry. Discard any remaining large pieces of fat.

6. Taste the pork to check for seasoning and add salt, pepper, and lime juice as necessary.

7. Serve hot, with corn tortillas, guacamole, and pico de gallo or salsa. Leftovers can be refrigerated in a covered container for up to 2 days.

TIP

- **To make the meal ahead of time, stop after Step 4. Remove the meat from the skillet and transfer it to a covered container, leaving behind the fat. Pour the fat into a covered glass container. Refrigerate both for up to 2 days. When ready to serve, melt the fat over medium heat, then add the pork and continue with Step 5.**

Shakshuka

The bright red of the tomato-pepper sauce and the rich yellow of the egg yolks are an invitation to dive into the skillet.

Time: 45 minutes
Yield: Serves 2

This dish appears to have its origins in North Africa or the Middle East. And, of course, there are people who have known about shakshuka for a good long time. But shakshuka has experienced a recent burst in popularity, and I have a theory that could just explain that: It combines familiar and accessible ingredients. It's really good. And it gives you permission to eat eggs for dinner. (As if any were needed.)

There's a reluctance sometimes to cook with tomatoes in cast iron—the idea being that their acid eats away at the seasoning or the dish takes on a metallic taste. That may be a danger if your tomatoes are in the skillet for hours. Fortunately, this dish is ready in much less time.

INGREDIENTS

2 tablespoons olive oil

1¼ cups diced white or yellow onion (about 1 medium-size onion)

1 clove garlic, minced

1½ cups diced green or red bell pepper (about 1 large pepper)

1 (28-ounce) can diced tomatoes

2 tablespoons tomato paste

Chili powder

1 teaspoon ground cumin

1 teaspoon sweet paprika

¼ teaspoon freshly ground black pepper

Salt

4 large eggs

Chopped fresh parsley or cilantro, for garnish

Cooked rice or couscous, or sliced baguette, for serving (optional)

Shakshuka, page 125

1 Preheat the skillet over medium heat for 2 minutes. Add the olive oil, then add the onion and cook, stirring occasionally, until it begins to soften, about 3 minutes. Add the garlic and continue to cook until fragrant, about 1 minute.

2 Add the bell pepper and cook, stirring occasionally, until softened, about 5 minutes.

3 Add the tomatoes with their juice, the tomato paste, a pinch of chili powder, the cumin, and the paprika. Stir until well mixed. Let the mixture simmer, stirring occasionally, until it has reduced slightly, about 10 minutes. Add the black pepper, then taste to check for seasoning and add salt and chili powder as necessary. Be cautious with both; once they're in the dish, there's no getting them back out.

4 Crack the eggs over the tomato mixture, spacing them evenly. Turn the heat to medium low and loosely cover the skillet with aluminum foil or a lid left slightly ajar. Allow to simmer until the tomatoes have reduced a bit more and the eggs are cooked, about 10 minutes.

5 Uncover the skillet, remove from the heat, and transfer it to a rack to cool slightly, about 5 minutes. Garnish with parsley and serve hot, on its own, atop rice or couscous, or accompanied by slices of baguette. Leftovers can be refrigerated in a covered container for up to 2 days.

Variations

- *In Step 3, stir in 1 cup crumbled feta cheese (about 5 ounces) before checking for seasoning.*

- *Want to stretch the meal to serve more people? Add up to 4 more eggs and serve with Fainá (page 61) or Salt-Roasted Potatoes (page 77) and a green salad.*

TIP

- **For a picture-perfect shakshuka, make a dent in the sauce with the back of a spoon to provide a space for each egg to land, and avoid a broken yolk by first cracking each egg into a ramekin, then gently pouring the egg into the tomato mixture.**

Seared Rib Eye Steak with Skillet Sauce

Time: 20 minutes
Yield: Serves 2

The outside of the meat is nicely browned in the skillet before the juices help to create a shallot and cider sauce.

Ventilation is key here. These steaks will develop a beautiful crust, but they're going to give off some smoke in the process. Now let's talk steak temperatures: If you don't have a thermometer, make a tiny cut to look inside the steak to see how much pink remains. Are there tricks to avoid this? Some, yes. But how confident are you in those tricks? Anyone eating the steak is certainly going to know how pink it is—you probably should, too. Making a small incision and, in this case, serving it with a skillet sauce mean no one needs to know you peeked.

Steak temperatures have a certain momentum. If you find the steak, say, rare and you're looking for medium, you may want to check again in as little as 30 seconds. Don't let more than 1 minute pass before you check again. It's a difference of about 15°F, and those degrees tick away very quickly in a hot skillet.

Some pan sauces use red wine to deglaze the pan, but here we swap in hard cider.

INGREDIENTS

2 boneless rib eye steaks, 1 inch thick (about 6 ounces each)

Salt and freshly ground black pepper

1 teaspoon neutral-flavored oil (such as canola or peanut)

1 shallot, minced

¼ cup hard cider (see Note)

2 tablespoons unsalted butter

- *Hard cider should be dry—that is, not too sweet.*

1 Place two oven-safe dinner plates on a rack in the oven and preheat the oven on its lowest setting.

2 Use paper towels to pat the steaks dry. Season both sides of each steak with salt and pepper.

3 Add the oil to the skillet and heat over medium high until the oil is just beginning to smoke, about 3 minutes.

4 Add the steaks to the skillet and cook until the bottoms are well browned, about 3 minutes. Flip the steaks and continue cooking until the other side is well browned, about 3 minutes more. If you have an instant-read thermometer, use it to check the temperature of the steaks. For a steak cooked medium-rare, the temperature should be 130°F; well done is 155°F. If you do not have an instant-read thermometer, make an incision in the top of a steak about ½-inch deep. For a steak done medium, you should see no red but some pink in the center. If the steak needs more cooking time, flip it again and cook for 1 minute before checking. Remove the steaks just shy of your preferred doneness, as they will continue to cook just a bit as they rest.

5 Place the steaks on plates, cover them with foil, and allow them to rest at room temperature while you make the skillet sauce.

6 Turn the heat to low, add the shallot to the skillet and cook until it is softened, about 1 minute. Stir in the cider and cook until reduced slightly, about 30 seconds. Remove the skillet from the heat, add the butter, and swirl the skillet to melt it. Season with salt and pepper to taste.

7 Serve the steaks hot, drizzling some of the sauce over them and serving the rest on the side.

Variations

- *Add 1 sprig fresh thyme with the cider in Step 6. Remove it before serving.*

- *Substitute an equal amount of reduced-sodium vegetable, chicken, or beef broth for the hard cider.*

TIP
- **When it comes to determining whether a steak is done to your liking, there's no substitute for an instant-read thermometer. They can be pricey, but a good one lasts a long time. And having an instant digital read-out of your food's temperature with just a quick poke is unbeatable.**

Couscous with Apricots and Cashews

Time: 20 minutes
Yield: Serves 4

Aluminum foil keeps the moisture in as the couscous cooks, while nuts and dried fruit keep this between savory and sweet territory.

Couscous looks a little like barley but isn't a grain in its own right—couscous is made from the same semolina flour as dried pasta. It's much smaller than most pasta shapes, though, which means it doesn't need the same high heat to hydrate.

Most of the cooking here takes place off the heat. Many recipes call for adding boiling water to the couscous, but this recipe takes a different tack: Gently cooking the dried apricots in the olive oil first infuses the oil with the fragrance of the fruit and allows the oil to carry it through the dish. By the time the couscous and water are added, the skillet has enough retained warmth to heat the water. Just cover the skillet to let the couscous absorb the water, and 10 minutes later it's done.

INGREDIENTS

2 tablespoons extra-virgin olive oil

1/4 cup coarsely chopped dried apricots

1/4 cup whole salted roasted cashews, coarsely chopped

1 cup couscous

Salt

1 1/4 cups water or unsalted chicken broth

Freshly ground black pepper

1 Preheat the skillet over medium heat for 2 minutes.

2 Turn the heat to medium low. Add the olive oil and apricots. Cook, stirring occasionally, until the apricots are fragrant and just starting to brown, about 5 minutes.

Couscous with Apricots and Cashews, page 131

3 Add the cashews, couscous, and ½ teaspoon salt. Pour in the water. Stir with a fork to combine, then cover tightly with aluminum foil or a lid and remove from the heat.

4 Let the skillet sit off the heat for 10 minutes, then uncover it, fluff the couscous with a fork, and season to taste with salt and pepper before serving. Leftovers can be refrigerated in a covered container for up to 2 days.

Variations

- *Substitute dried cranberries or cherries for the apricots.*

- *Substitute salted roasted almonds for the cashews.*

TIP

- **To make cutting sticky dried fruit easier, spray your knife with a little nonstick cooking spray or wipe it on a paper towel moistened with oil.**

Gnocchi with Goat Cheese and Skillet-Roasted Tomatoes

Time: 2 hours
Yield: Serves 2

If you've had only boiled gnocchi, you're in for a treat when you taste them dappled with goat cheese and combined with canned tomatoes roasted in the skillet.

Here's a revelation: Even canned tomatoes benefit from the flavor concentration that takes place during roasting.

So if you're making your gnocchi from scratch and you're going to have the oven on to bake the potato anyway, why not throw the tomatoes in the skillet and get a little char on them?

Of course, making gnocchi from scratch isn't always in the cards. The recipe works with packaged gnocchi, too (see Variation).

It's still worth roasting the tomatoes if you can swing it—it takes about an hour but doesn't require your attention.

When it comes to cooking the gnocchi in the skillet, covering it at first allows the gnocchi to get a jump on cooking and heat through, while removing the cover for the final few minutes means they brown nicely.

Once the goat cheese is added off the heat, it melds with the tomatoes and turns into an instant creamy sauce.

INGREDIENTS

1 (28-ounce) can whole peeled plum tomatoes, drained

3 tablespoons extra-virgin olive oil, plus more for garnish

1 large russet potato (about 12 ounces)

¼ cup unbleached all-purpose flour, plus more for kneading

Salt and freshly ground black pepper

3 ounces mild soft goat cheese, broken into small pieces

Fresh basil leaves, for garnish

NOTE

- *Save the liquid from the drained tomatoes in a zip-top freezer bag or covered container in the freezer. Substitute it for some of the cooking water for pasta that will be served with a tomato-based sauce, add it to stew or soup, or use it to cook rice.*

1 Preheat the oven to 350°F with one rack in the middle.

2 Line the skillet with parchment paper. Cut the canned tomatoes in half lengthwise and spread them on the skillet. Don't overlap the tomatoes. If you have more than will fit, set the extras aside to add in Step 9. Drizzle the tomatoes with 1 tablespoon of the olive oil.

3 Place the skillet in the oven. Pierce the potato with a fork and place it directly on the oven rack. Bake until the tomatoes are shriveled and the potato is easily pierced with a fork, about 1 hour 15 minutes.

4 Remove the skillet and the potato from the oven. Chop the tomatoes into bite-size pieces and set aside. Remove and discard the parchment paper from the skillet.

5 Let the potato cool slightly, then peel it. Pass the potato through a food mill or a ricer, or grate it through the large holes of a box grater, into a large bowl. Add the flour and use your hands to mix them together, breaking up any lumps of potato along the way. Sprinkle ½ teaspoon salt and ¼ teaspoon pepper over the dough and knead lightly to distribute evenly.

6 Gently knead the dough a few times to bring it together. It should be moist, but not wet and sticky. If it's too sticky, add 1 tablespoon flour at a time.

7 Dust a work surface lightly with flour and turn out the dough onto it. Roll the dough into a log and cut it into 2 pieces. Roll each piece of dough into a rope about the diameter of your thumb. Use a sharp knife to cut it into 1-inch segments. Gently press each segment between your finger and a fork, leaving a fork mark on one side.

8 Preheat the skillet over medium heat for 1 minute. Add 2 tablespoons olive oil, then the gnocchi. Cover tightly with a lid or aluminum foil and cook for 3 minutes. Remove the lid and cook, stirring occasionally, until the gnocchi are golden brown in spots, about 3 minutes.

9 Remove the skillet from the heat, add the tomatoes and goat cheese, and gently stir until the goat cheese is melted.

10 Taste to check for seasoning and add salt and pepper as necessary. Serve hot, drizzled with olive oil and garnished with basil leaves. Leftovers can be refrigerated in a covered container for up to 2 days.

Variation

- *Starting with packaged gnocchi? Omit the potato and flour and skip Steps 5 through 7.*

Okonomiyaki

Traditionally cooked at a grill set into the table or counter, this savory Japanese pancake is a natural for the skillet.

Time: 30 minutes
Yield: Serves 4

I wish I could tell you that I am a student of Japanese cuisine. I'm not.

I am, however, a master of eating just about everything put in front of me. A few times when I've been in Japan, what's been put in front of me has been *okonomiyaki*.

There are different styles that vary by region, and the idea of one true okonomiyaki recipe is like having the one true pizza recipe—good luck with that. It depends on the style you're after. It depends on the toppings you want. It depends—and this part is key—on what you have on hand. So consider this recipe a blueprint and feel free to tinker.

Okonomiyaki is typically cooked on a hot griddle, which can be anywhere from personal-size to counter-length. Your skillet is more on the personal-size end of the continuum, and it works quite well for this.

In Japan, okonomiyaki sauce is easy to find in the supermarket and people aren't any more likely to make it themselves than I would be to make, say, ketchup. But where I live, the reality is that even in Asian markets it can be tricky to find, so it's good to know you can use ingredients you might already have to make a sweet and umami-loaded sauce.

INGREDIENTS

1 cup unbleached all-purpose flour

3 scallions, green and white parts finely chopped separately

3¹/₂ cups shredded cabbage (about half a small head)

¹/₂ cup water

3 large eggs

¹/₂ teaspoon salt

1 teaspoon neutral-flavored oil (such as canola or peanut)

6 strips bacon

Toasted sesame seeds, chopped scallion greens, Okonomiyaki Sauce (recipe follows, or store-bought), and mayonnaise, for serving

NOTE

- *Cole slaw mix is often sold near the salad greens in the supermarket and can be substituted for the cabbage in equal volume.*

1 Preheat the oven on its lowest setting. (This allows you to keep the first okonomiyaki warm while you finish the second.)

2 In a large bowl, combine the flour, the white parts of the scallions, and the cabbage. In a small bowl, combine the water, eggs, and salt. Add the wet ingredients to the flour and vegetables and stir gently, only enough to bring everything together.

3 Place the skillet over medium-high heat, add the oil to the skillet, and heat until it's hot but not smoking, about 2 minutes. Add half the batter and push it down with a spatula to flatten into a thick pancake, leaving about ¹/₂ inch of the pan visible around the batter. (This will give your spatula room to slide under later.) Turn the heat to medium and cook until the underside is browned, about 4 minutes.

4 Place 3 strips of the bacon atop the pancake. You may need to cut or bend the bacon so it fits. Flip the pancake so that the bacon is touching the skillet. If the pancake comes apart when you flip it, don't worry—use a spatula to herd any stray parts back together. Cook until the bacon is crisp (lift the edge of the pancake with a spatula to check) and no uncooked egg remains, about 5 minutes more.

5 Place the finished okonomiyaki on a plate and move it into the oven to keep it warm.

6 Repeat Steps 3 through 5 with the remaining batter and bacon. Because of the bacon fat, you probably won't need to add more oil. In fact, depending on how much bacon fat is in the skillet, you may need to pour some off before continuing.

7 Cut the okonomiyaki into quarters and top with sesame seeds and scallion greens. In Japan, the sauce and mayonnaise are often drizzled with a squeeze bottle in a zig-zag pattern over the okonomiyaki, but you may also serve them on the side. Leftovers can be refrigerated in a covered container for up to 2 days.

TIP

- **When it comes to flipping the okonomiyaki, one swift and fluid motion is best. Tentative poking around gives the whole thing more opportunity to fall apart. Okonomiyaki can sense fear, so be fearless and just go for it.**

Variation

- *Replace the shredded cabbage with an equal amount of shredded broccoli stalks, sometimes available as broccoli slaw in the produce section.*

Okonomiyaki Sauce

Time: **5 minutes**

Yield: **About 1/3 cup**

Pro tip for when you're measuring out ingredients for this umami-soaked sauce: A drop of oil rubbed on the measuring spoon or a quick spritz of nonstick cooking spray makes measuring honey much easier—it slides out rather than sticking.

INGREDIENTS

2 tablespoons Worcestershire sauce

3 tablespoons honey

1 teaspoon ketchup

1/2 teaspoon grated fresh ginger

NOTE

- *Peel the ginger first. Do it the easy way: Use a spoon to scrape off its outermost layer.*

In a small bowl, combine all of the ingredients and mix well with a fork.

Seafood Paella

Originally cooked over an open flame in a shallow pan, this dish from Spain's Valencia region fits right into your skillet.

Time: 45 minutes
Yield: Serves 4

There's no question that authentic paella is not made in a skillet. And there are a practically uncountable number of paellas in Spain, all with varying ingredients and regional twists. Chicken, rabbit, and escargots all have a claim to being a part of traditional paella.

For the skillet, my thoughts turned to a seafood-based paella, with chicken broth and saffron to tie the dish back to its origins. There are substitutes for saffron, but—and this is key—they really seek only to replicate the distinct yellow hue it lends a dish. Nothing can mimic its flavor.

Skillet paella takes advantage of cast iron's versatility. It starts on the stovetop and finishes in the oven, which means the last 30 minutes or so don't require you to hover over the dish and leaves you free to enjoy, say, a traditional Spanish beverage such as sangria, or the drink of your choice. We already agreed we weren't being sticklers here, right?

INGREDIENTS

3 cups reduced-sodium chicken broth

1 tablespoon tomato paste

Pinch of whole saffron threads (optional; see Notes)

3 tablespoons extra-virgin olive oil

1 medium-size white or yellow onion, finely chopped

1 1/2 cups Arborio rice (see Notes)

1 medium-size plum tomato, diced

Salt and freshly ground black pepper

1 pound raw scallops and/or peeled shrimp and/or squid, cut into 1-inch chunks

Chopped fresh parsley and lemon wedges, for garnish

NOTES

- *Saffron is expensive, yes, but also irreplaceable—and note how little is required. A small vial will carry you through quite a few recipes. What you're buying are the hand-harvested stigmas of a crocus flower, which lends not only a bright yellow color to the dish but also an almost sweet, floral background note that might be compared very roughly to a cup of Earl Grey tea. It can be added to rice dishes, stews, and soups.*

- *Arborio rice is not the traditional rice for paella—but neither is a cast-iron skillet the traditional vessel. Arborio does share an important trait with the bomba variety of rice typically used, in that it will stay distinct and not turn to mush, even as it absorbs the liquid around it.*

1 Preheat the oven to 450°F with one rack in the middle.

2 In the skillet over medium heat, warm up about ½ cup of the broth to about 120°F (the temperature of hot tap water) for about 2 minutes. In a small bowl, mix the tomato paste with the warm broth and saffron. Allow the mixture to stand. (This allows the color and flavor of the saffron to be more evenly distributed when it's added to the rest of the broth and the rice. If you're not using the saffron, don't skip this step; it also helps the tomato paste disperse evenly in the skillet.)

3 Turn the heat to medium high, add the olive oil to the skillet, and allow it to heat for 1 minute. Add the onion and cook, stirring occasionally, until it's softened, about 5 minutes.

4 Add the rice and cook, stirring frequently, until it turns shiny, about 2 minutes.

5 Taking care because the skillet is hot (and the liquid may bubble and spit), add all of the broth to the skillet, including the warmed broth with the saffron, followed by the tomato.

6 Add ¼ teaspoon salt and ¼ teaspoon pepper, stir, then taste to check for seasoning and add more salt and pepper as necessary.

7 Stir in the seafood, then place the skillet in the oven.

8 Bake until almost all the liquid is absorbed, about 30 minutes.

9 Remove the skillet from the oven and serve the paella hot, garnished with parsley and lemon wedges. Leftovers can be refrigerated in a covered container for 1 day.

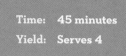

Scallop Risotto

Searing the scallops in the skillet before preparing the risotto turns them golden brown and perfumes the dish.

Risotto has a reputation as a labor-intensive dish. And it's true that it does require some attention and stirring. But it's not something that requires a magic touch or special equipment. Would you believe a skillet will do the job? (Surely at this point in the book your answer to that is a confident "Yes.")

Scallops cook in practically no time at all, so one of the tricks to making this work is to quickly cook the scallops and then set them aside while the risotto slowly absorbs the liquid, adding the scallops back only at the end to gently rewarm them.

INGREDIENTS

4 tablespoons (1/2 stick) unsalted butter

1 pound small scallops (60 to 80 per pound), patted dry (see Notes)

Salt and freshly ground black pepper

Grated zest and juice of 1 lemon (see Tips)

1 medium-size white or yellow onion, minced

1 1/2 cups Arborio rice

6 cups reduced-sodium chicken broth, heated to about 120°F (see Notes)

1/4 cup freshly grated Parmesan cheese

Chopped fresh parsley or thyme, for garnish

NOTES

- *Scallop sizes are determined by how many make up a pound. Thus, "60 to 80" scallops are smaller than those labeled "40 to 60." Scallops of sizes other than "60 to 80" can be used, but avoid anything larger than 20 to 40 per pound—bigger than that won't be bite-size.*

- *It's not necessary to dig out the thermometer to measure the temperature of the broth—just heat it to the temperature of very hot tap water. The risotto will come together a bit more quickly if you hold it at that temperature, but if you're not able to, it's fine to let the broth cool off slightly as you make the risotto—just allow an extra*

Scallop Risotto, page 145

*minute or so for the broth to heat up after
you add it to the skillet.*

1 Preheat the skillet over medium-high heat for 2 minutes.

2 Place 1 tablespoon of butter in the skillet. While the butter melts, sprinkle the scallops with ¼ teaspoon salt and ¼ teaspoon pepper. Add the scallops to the skillet and cook, stirring occasionally, until browned, about 4 minutes. If the scallops release liquid and do not brown, it's okay; just cook the scallops until they are opaque, about 4 minutes. The liquid released by the scallops can remain in the skillet. Using a slotted spoon, place the scallops on a plate and set aside.

3 Turn the heat to medium and add 1 tablespoon of the butter and the lemon juice. Add the onion, ¼ teaspoon salt, and ¼ teaspoon pepper and cook until the onion is softened, about 5 minutes.

4 Add the rice, stir to coat it with the butter and onions, and cook until the grains turn opaque, about 2 minutes.

5 Turn the heat to medium low and add about 1 cup of the broth. Stir frequently until the rice has absorbed all of the liquid, about 5 minutes. Add another cup of the broth and continue cooking and stirring until this broth is absorbed, about 5 minutes. Repeat twice more.

6 After adding 4 cups broth, taste the risotto. The grains of rice should have a bit of resistance and the dish overall should be creamy. If the grains are too firm, add another cup of broth and continue to cook, stirring, until the liquid is absorbed. Taste the risotto again and add the final cup of broth if needed.

7 Remove the risotto from the stove and fold in the remaining 2 tablespoons butter, the Parmesan, and the lemon zest. Fold in the scallops. Taste one last time for seasoning and add salt and pepper as necessary.

8 Serve hot, garnished with parsley. Leftovers can be refrigerated in a covered container for 1 day.

TIPS

- **Freeze any unused broth in easy-to-use cubes: Pour the broth into an ice cube tray and freeze. Once frozen, store the cubes in a zip-top freezer bag.**
- **For an extra lemony note, grate the lemon zest onto the serving plates before adding it in Step 7. The plates will retain the lemon fragrance when the risotto is served.**

Chicken Potpie (in a Skillet)

Time: 45 minutes
Yield: Serves 4

This version skips a traditional crust
and gets crowned with a buttery, crumbly cracker topping.

'm a fan of cooking from scratch, but I've certainly fished my fair share of dinners out of the freezer case. I have a soft spot for those packaged chicken potpies, with their double crusts, mechanically perfect cubes of carrot and potatoes, frozen peas, and occasional piece of chicken.

This recipe will not have you missing the chicken. There's plenty.

Making everything in the skillet means no crust on the bottom, since the sauce and all of the filling ingredients are cooked together on the stovetop. You won't find the traditional crust on top, either. Instead, crushed crackers add crunch there.

INGREDIENTS

Topping

25 saltine crackers

3 tablespoons freshly grated Parmesan cheese

1/8 teaspoon dried ground sage

3 tablespoons unsalted butter, melted

Filling

2 tablespoons unsalted butter

1 cup diced white or yellow onion (about 1 small onion)

3/4 cup diced celery (about 2 large stalks, trimmed)

1 1/2 cups reduced-sodium chicken broth

1 cup milk

1/3 cup unbleached all-purpose flour

1/2 teaspoon dried thyme

1/4 teaspoon salt

1/4 teaspoon freshly ground black pepper

2 1/2 cups chopped cooked chicken (about 12 ounces)

1 cup frozen peas

1. Make the topping: In a small bowl, finely crush the crackers. Stir in the Parmesan and sage. Add the butter and mix with a fork until the ingredients are evenly distributed. Set aside.

2. Preheat the oven to 400°F with one rack in the middle. Preheat the skillet over medium heat for 2 minutes.

3. Make the filling: Add the butter to the skillet and allow it to melt, then add the onion and celery. Cook, stirring occasionally, until the onions soften, about 10 minutes.

4. In a small bowl or measuring cup, combine the broth and milk. In another small bowl, combine the flour, thyme, salt, and pepper, then sprinkle the mixture into the skillet. Gradually whisk in the broth and milk, adding about a quarter of the total liquid at a time and whisking until the mixture thickens before adding more. The first batch of liquid should thicken almost instantly, though it may take as long as 5 minutes to add and thicken all of the liquid. When all of the liquid has been added, stir in the chicken and peas and remove the skillet from the heat.

5. Sprinkle the topping over the skillet and place it in the oven. Bake until the topping is beginning to brown and the liquid is bubbling around the edges, about 10 minutes.

6. Remove the skillet from the oven and transfer it to a rack to cool slightly, about 10 minutes. Serve hot. Leftovers can be refrigerated in a covered container for up to 2 days.

Variation

- *Substitute 2 cups cubed cooked ham for the chicken and omit the salt. (The ham has a more assertive flavor, so slightly less is needed.)*

CHAPTER 5

Desserts

Giant Chocolate Chip Skillet Cookie

Time: 45 minutes
Cool: 1 hour
Yield: Serves 16

Quick! Eat this cookie before it eats you! I'm kidding, but why take chances? This is one big cookie.

Have you ever looked at a plate of chocolate chip cookies and thought, "Wow, I could dive right into that"? No need to answer out loud.

Here's a cookie that you really can dive into, although a fork and knife would perhaps bring a modicum of social acceptance.

The real key in developing this recipe was to decide if mixing the ingredients in the skillet would work, or if it would be necessary to use separate bowls, as in a traditional recipe. In general, creaming the butter and sugar together creates air bubbles and makes the cookie more cake-like, while mixing the sugar into melted butter leads to a denser, chewier cookie. Now, of course, some of this comes down to preference. On the other hand, no one

I know has a preference for doing more dishes, so the all-in-the-skillet method had a clear edge. Fortunately, it also makes a great cookie.

INGREDIENTS

10 tablespoons (1¼ sticks) unsalted butter

2/3 cup firmly packed light brown sugar

1/3 cup granulated sugar

2 teaspoons vanilla extract

1 large egg plus 1 large egg yolk

1¾ cups unbleached all-purpose flour

1/2 teaspoon baking soda

1/4 teaspoon baking powder

1/4 teaspoon salt

3/4 cup semisweet or bittersweet chocolate chips

1. Preheat the oven to 350°F with one rack in the middle.

2. Over medium-low heat, melt the butter in the skillet. Remove the skillet from the heat and stir in the brown sugar, granulated sugar, and vanilla. Allow to cool for 5 minutes.

3. Add the egg and egg yolk to the skillet, first by gently whisking to break up the yolks, then by whisking more vigorously and dragging the whisk along the edges of the skillet to fully incorporate them.

4. In a small bowl, stir together the flour, baking soda, baking powder, and salt. Add the mixture to the skillet in four batches, whisking each time until very few streaks of flour remain; for the last batch, switch to a spatula. Fold the chocolate chips into the batter. Do not overmix; it's okay if a few streaks of flour remain.

5. Use the spatula to press the dough into an even layer. Place the skillet in the oven and bake until the surface is golden brown, but the center is still soft, about 25 minutes.

6. Remove the skillet from the oven and transfer it to a rack to cool until just warm, about 1 hour. Cut into wedges and serve warm or at room temperature. Leftovers can be stored for 1 day at room temperature in the skillet, covered loosely with plastic wrap. Slices can be frozen in a zip-top bag for up to 3 months.

Waffle Bread Pudding

Here's an unfussy ending to a meal that takes advantage of the skillet to showcase the contrast between the soft, custardy middle and the lightly crunchy edges.

I f you're a certain type of person, you'll insist on tearing the waffles along the grid lines—not that there's any right way to do it. (It all tastes the same, naturally.) No matter how the waffles are torn, though, the geometry and the presentation here are special while the flavors—waffles, butter, and maple syrup—are familiar. Setting aside a little butter to grease the skillet ensures the pudding lifts out easily. Meanwhile, the skillet creates such a beautiful contrast of textures: crunchy at the edges and so soft in the middle.

INGREDIENTS

Unsalted butter, softened, for greasing the skillet

2½ cups milk (see Notes)

4 tablespoons (½ stick) unsalted butter, melted

3 large eggs

½ cup maple syrup

¼ teaspoon salt

8 Belgian-style toaster waffles, thawed at room temperature

1 tablespoon sugar

Maple syrup, for serving (optional)

NOTES

- *Use whole milk if available.*

- *Belgian-style waffles are thicker and more substantial than their regular counterparts. In a pinch, you can do a 2-for-1 substitution and use 16 regular toaster waffles.*

1 Preheat the oven to 350°F with one rack in the middle. Using your finger or a piece of butter wrapper, thoroughly coat the bottom and sides of the skillet with a thin layer of butter.

2 In a large bowl, whisk together the milk, melted butter, eggs, maple syrup, and salt until combined.

3 Slice or tear the waffles into bite-size pieces. Submerge the waffle pieces in the milk mixture for 5 minutes, stirring occasionally to make sure the liquid is absorbed evenly. At first, some pieces will poke up above the liquid; they will sink as the pieces below soften and are stirred.

4 Pour the soaked waffles and any remaining liquid into the skillet and sprinkle with the sugar.

5 Place the skillet in the oven and bake until a knife inserted in the center comes out clean, about 45 minutes. The center may still be a bit wobbly but will set as the pudding cools.

6 Remove the skillet from the oven and transfer it to a rack to cool slightly before serving, about 15 minutes. Serve warm with maple syrup if desired. Leftovers can be refrigerated in a covered container for up to 2 days. (Like cold pizza, cold Waffle Bread Pudding has its devotees but may not be for everyone.)

Variation

- *In Step 4, dust the top with ¼ teaspoon ground cinnamon in addition to the sugar.*

Waffle Bread Pudding, page 155

Rice Pudding

Few desserts can feel as right on a hot day as on a cold day.

Time: 1 hour
30 minutes
Yield: Serves 4

This rice pudding is lightly sweet and comforting when served warm. Served cold, it's refreshing and slightly less sweet. (The amount of sugar hasn't changed, but we don't perceive sweet things the same when they're warm as when they're cold; for proof, try drinking melted, room-temperature ice cream—it's almost unbearably sweet.)

My big concern going into this was whether the rice or the milk would burn in the skillet. As it turns out, cooking the rice first in water and then on gentle heat with the milk means that the milk doesn't have a chance to scorch.

INGREDIENTS

1½ cups water

¼ teaspoon salt

½ tablespoon unsalted butter

½ cup Arborio rice

2 cups milk (see Notes)

¼ cup sugar

1 cinnamon stick (about 2 inches long; see Notes)

1 teaspoon vanilla extract

Ground cinnamon, for serving

NOTES

- *Use whole milk if available. The richness of this dish relies in part on the creaminess of the milk.*

- *No cinnamon stick? Substitute with ¼ teaspoon ground cinnamon. The pudding will take on a slightly darker color.*

1 Over medium heat, bring the water, salt, and butter to a boil in the skillet. Add the rice, return to a boil, and turn the heat to low. Cook, stirring occasionally, until the rice has absorbed the water, 20 to 30 minutes.

2 Add the milk, sugar, and cinnamon stick to the skillet. Simmer over medium-low heat, stirring occasionally, until the rice is soft, but not mushy, and the mixture has thickened, 30 to 45 minutes.

3 Stir in the vanilla, remove the cinnamon stick, and allow the pudding to cool slightly. If a skin forms on the top as it cools, just stir it back into the pudding. Serve warm, or transfer to a bowl, cover, and allow to cool in the refrigerator. Dust lightly with the ground cinnamon just before serving. Leftovers can be refrigerated in a covered container for up to 2 days.

Variations

- *Add the grated zest of 1 lemon at the beginning of the cooking time in Step 2.*

- *Add ¼ cup raisins, dried cranberries, or dried cherries after 15 minutes of cooking in Step 2.*

Pluot Clafoutis

Traditionally made with cherries, this French cross between a pancake and a custard bakes up fluffy in the skillet with a sweet-tart edge from the fruit.

Time: 1 hour
Yield: 8 slices

First off: It's pronounced, roughly, "clah-foo-TEE," not "clah-FOO-tee," which is disappointing only because, pronounced correctly, it sounds just slightly less like something out of a Dr. Seuss book.

In general it's better to concern oneself with how a dessert tastes on the palate than how it rolls off the tongue, but the name of this dessert has brought me an embarrassing amount of joy over the years. And the words still bring a smile to my face.

So what's a pluot? It's a cross between a plum and an apricot.

My key finding was that all but the most well-seasoned of skillets will benefit from a little butter to help the clafoutis lift out at the end.

INGREDIENTS

½ cup unbleached all-purpose flour

3 tablespoons granulated sugar

Pinch of salt

1 cup milk

2 large eggs

2 tablespoons unsalted butter, melted and cooled

¼ teaspoon vanilla extract

Unsalted butter, softened, for greasing the skillet

5 medium-size pluots, pitted and sliced into eighths

Confectioners' sugar, for serving

1 Preheat the oven to 350°F with one rack in the middle.

2 In a medium-size bowl, stir together the flour, granulated sugar, and salt.

3 Measure the milk in a large measuring cup, then use a fork to beat in the eggs, melted butter, and vanilla. Add to the flour mixture and whisk until smooth.

4 Using your finger or a piece of butter wrapper, coat the bottom and sides of the skillet with a thin layer of softened butter.

5 Spread the pluots in a single layer across the bottom of the skillet. Pour the batter on top of the fruit.

6 Place the skillet in the oven and bake until the clafoutis is puffed and browned and a knife inserted in the center comes out clean, about 45 minutes. If your pluots are particularly juicy, it could take up to another 15 minutes to cook through.

7 Remove the skillet from the oven and and transfer it to a rack to cool slightly, about 10 minutes. The clafoutis will deflate as it cools.

8 Slice and serve warm, dusted with confectioners' sugar. Leftovers can be refrigerated in a covered container for up to 2 days.

Variations

- *Sour cherries are the canonical clafoutis fruit. Substitute 2 cups pitted sour cherries for the pluots.*

- *Can't find pluots? You can keep it in the same family and use plums or apricots instead—or create your own hybrid clafoutis and use equal parts of each.*

Pluot Clafoutis, page 161

Chocolate Cake

No cake pans? No problem.

Time: 30 minutes
Cool: 30 minutes
Yield: Serves 8

With practice I've become better, but there have definitely been times when my cake attempts came out looking like the fun house mirror version of the camera-ready incarnation on the cookbook page.

So my vision for this was a simple, no-frills cake that comes together with minimum fuss, and with things you're likely to have on hand. So, no cake flour. No espresso powder. No bricks of unsweetened chocolate. (Those are all part of many great chocolate cakes; they're just not part of this one.)

Serving it from the skillet means there's no need to fuss with greasing or flouring a cake pan. (I tried it both ways and it made only the slightest difference.) The only question was whether the skillet's heat retention would mean the cake burned or cooked too quickly. The key turned out to be baking at a slightly lower temperature than a typical cake.

INGREDIENTS

1 cup unbleached all-purpose flour

3/4 cup sugar

1/2 cup unsweetened cocoa powder

1 teaspoon baking powder

3/4 teaspoon baking soda

1/2 teaspoon salt

1/4 cup neutral-flavored oil (such as canola or peanut)

1 large egg plus 1 large egg yolk

2 teaspoons vanilla extract

1 cup boiling water

Vanilla ice cream, for serving

1 Preheat the oven to 325°F with one rack in the middle.

2 In a large bowl, whisk together the flour, sugar, cocoa, baking powder, baking soda, and salt.

3 In a small bowl, whisk the oil, egg, egg yolk, and vanilla. Whisk this into the dry ingredients. The mixture may be clumpy and stick to the whisk; that's okay.

4 While whisking gently, carefully add the water. Whisk vigorously for 1 minute, until the water is completely incorporated.

5 Pour the batter into the skillet and place in the oven. Bake for 25 minutes, then check for doneness by inserting a toothpick into the center of the cake. The toothpick should emerge just slightly wet toward the tip, with only a few crumbs attached. If it's too wet, allow the cake to bake for another 3 minutes, then test again. (The edge of the cake will set first; a toothpick inserted at the edge will emerge clean even if the center is not yet done.)

6 Remove the skillet from the oven and transfer it to a rack to cool until warm but not hot, about 30 minutes.

7 Run a sharp knife around the edge of the cake to separate it from the sides of the skillet, then use the knife to slice. Serve the cake warm, with vanilla ice cream. Leftovers can be stored for 1 day at room temperature in the skillet, covered loosely with plastic wrap. Slices can be frozen in a zip-top bag for up to 3 months.

TIP

- **There are three keys to making sure the soft, moist cake doesn't crumble as you slice: Wait until the cake has cooled a bit, use a sharp knife, and run that knife around the edge of the cake before cutting.**

Peanut Butter Swirl Brownies

No piles of dirty mixing bowls—everything happens in the skillet.

Time: 45 minutes
Cool: 45 minutes
Yield: 16 brownies

I f I'm making a sandwich or doing a stir-fry, I go for all-natural peanut butter—the kind that separates in the jar and needs to be refrigerated. So that's what I tried first for this recipe. I wanted to like it. But when I tried it with the other stuff—the stuff with a few extra ingredients, the stuff I grew up on—it worked so much better.

So while most of the time I live by the principle of "just peanuts," I had to slap some sense into myself this time around. We're dealing with brownies here—the extra fat and sugar in the peanut butter are not exactly what prevents this from being nature's most wholesome snack.

Sometimes you need a brownie. And your skillet is there for you.

INGREDIENTS

8 tablespoons (1 stick) unsalted butter

3 ounces unsweetened chocolate, coarsely chopped

1/2 cup granulated sugar

1/4 cup firmly packed light brown sugar

2 large eggs

2 teaspoons vanilla extract

1/2 cup unbleached all-purpose flour

1/4 teaspoon baking soda

1/2 cup smooth peanut butter

1/4 teaspoon coarse salt

1 Preheat the oven to 350°F with one rack in the middle.

2 Melt the butter in the skillet over low heat. When the butter has melted, add the chocolate and stir until it is partially melted, about 1 minute. Remove from the heat and continue to stir until the chocolate has melted completely, about 1 minute more. Whisk in the granulated sugar and brown sugar. Add the eggs, one at a time, whisking after each addition until smooth. Whisk in the vanilla.

3 In a small bowl, combine the flour and baking soda. Add it to the skillet and stir using a folding motion to incorporate the flour until just combined. Level the mixture so that it is distributed evenly in the skillet.

4 Use a soupspoon to drop evenly spaced dollops of peanut butter onto the brownie batter. To swirl the peanut butter mixture into the batter, drag a knife lightly through the peanut butter, leaving distinct streaks of peanut butter. Sprinkle the salt atop the batter.

5 Place the skillet in the oven and bake until a toothpick inserted halfway between the edge of the skillet and the center comes out mostly clean, 20 to 25 minutes. A few crumbs on the toothpick are okay, but it should not be wet; the center of the brownie will still be quite moist.

6 Remove the skillet from the oven and transfer it to a rack to cool until warm but not hot, about 45 minutes. Cut into squares or wedges and serve the brownies warm or at room temperature. Leftovers can be stored for 1 day at room temperature in the skillet, covered loosely with plastic wrap. Slices can be frozen in a zip-top freezer bag for up to 3 months.

Peanut Butter Swirl Brownies, page 167

Mixed Fruit Galette

The free-form tart dough envelops just about any fruit, while the skillet takes care of collecting any juices that might run out.

"Rustic," as it applies to food, can be used to cover up blunders, flaws, and laziness. (Ask me how I know.) So I hesitate to describe this galette as rustic, but the truth is that's what it is: the unfussy cousin of a perfectly formed tart, with ragged edges and a more forgiving dough.

It's often baked on a baking sheet, but using the skillet instead means any runoff from the fruit won't collect on the bottom of your oven. In fact, it can be brushed back on top of the fruit as a glaze, along with any butter that escapes from the pastry.

INGREDIENTS

Crust

1¼ cups unbleached all-purpose flour, plus more for dusting the work surface

2 tablespoons granulated sugar, plus more for dusting

¼ teaspoon salt

8 tablespoons (1 stick) cold unsalted butter, cubed

¼ cup ice water, plus more if needed

2 large egg yolks

1 tablespoon water

Filling

1 tablespoon cornstarch

1 tablespoon granulated sugar

Pinch of salt

2½ cups mixed fresh berries (strawberries sliced if large), chopped peaches, and/or apricots pitted and cut in half

Confectioners' sugar, for serving

- *Ice water is important! It's worth putting a few ice cubes in a glass of cold water and measuring the water from there.*

1 Make the crust: In a food processor or a large bowl, combine the flour with the sugar and salt. Add the butter and pulse until crumbs form and no large chunks of butter remain, or use your fingers to pinch the butter into smaller, flour-coated chunks. You can also use a fork to mash smaller pieces of butter against the side of the bowl to break them up.

2 If using a food processor, transfer the mixture to a large bowl. In a small bowl or measuring cup, use a fork to mix together the ice water and 1 of the egg yolks. Evenly sprinkle that liquid over the flour-and-butter mixture. Gather it together with your hands, gently massaging it to distribute the moisture. Press the dough together with your hands until large clumps hold together. Avoid overmixing, and don't worry if every last bit of flour isn't incorporated; a bit of loose flour around the edges is okay. Add up to 1 teaspoon additional ice water at a time if the mixture is too dry to come together.

3 Place the dough onto a piece of plastic wrap about 18 inches long. Wrap the dough and press it together to form a cohesive mass. Pat it into a disk and refrigerate it for 15 minutes.

4 Preheat the oven to 400°F with one rack in the middle.

5 Make the filling: In a large bowl (you can use the same bowl used for the pastry), combine the cornstarch, granulated sugar, and salt. Add the fruit and toss until coated.

6 Dust a work surface with flour. Remove the dough from the refrigerator, remove the plastic wrap, and dust the top of the dough with flour. Use a rolling pin to press the dough into a rough circle about 11 inches in diameter. Uneven edges are perfectly okay.

7 Using your hands, carefully transfer the pastry to the skillet. (It may be easier if you fold it in half first and then unfold it in the skillet; make sure the top is lightly dusted with flour so the dough won't stick to itself.) Once in the skillet, the pastry can run up along the edges at first; it will be folded down later. If the pastry tears, gently press it back together with your fingertips. Use a few drops of ice water as glue if necessary.

8 Using a slotted spoon, place the filling in the center of the pastry, leaving behind any juices in the bowl and allowing a border of about 2 inches of pastry (including any dough running up the sides).

Fold the pastry edges toward the center, just covering the edge of the fruit. The center of the galette should not be covered with pastry, and the edges will be uneven. Beat together the remaining egg yolk and the tablespoon of water, lightly brush the pastry with this egg wash, then lightly sprinkle the pastry with the granulated sugar.

9 Place the skillet in the oven and bake until the pastry is golden and the fruit is bubbly, about 35 minutes.

10 Remove the skillet from the oven and transfer it to a rack to cool until warm but not hot, about 45 minutes. Any melted butter or fruit juices pooled along the edges can be carefully brushed on top of the fruit. This is optional.

11 Slice the galette into wedges and dust with confectioners' sugar just before serving

warm or at room temperature. Leftovers can be stored for 1 day at room temperature in the skillet, covered loosely with plastic wrap. Slices can be frozen in a zip-top freezer bag for up to 3 months.

TIPS

- **Keeping the ingredients cold in Steps 1 and 2 is important. If you need to step away from the kitchen for a bit—or if your kitchen is particularly hot—it's worth stashing the bowl in the refrigerator to keep things cool.**
- **The pastry can be made ahead and stored, wrapped in plastic wrap, in the refrigerator for up to 2 days. Let it sit at room temperature for 10 to 15 minutes before rolling.**

Peach Cobbler

Time: 1 hour
Cool: 30 minutes
Yield: Serves 8

The skillet emerges from the oven with the fruit mixture hot and bubbling and the top crunchy and sweet.

At their peak, peaches are one of summer's greatest gifts. Depending on where you live, the season can be anywhere from a few weeks to a few months. No matter where you live, it's probably shorter than it should be. All the more reason to take advantage of them while they're around.

The rough-hewn skillet is the perfect match for the uneven top crust of the cobbler, dropped by the spoonful atop ripe peaches with just a little bit of sugar. (This is not a cloying, syrupy filling.)

INGREDIENTS

¾ cup sugar

2 tablespoons cornstarch

½ teaspoon ground cinnamon

6 cups peeled and sliced peaches (about 6 medium-size peaches, cut into eighths)

½ cup unbleached all-purpose flour

½ teaspoon baking powder

Pinch of salt

8 tablespoons (1 stick) cold unsalted butter, cut into small chunks

1 large egg, beaten

1 teaspoon vanilla extract

NOTE

- *Peel peaches the easy way: Use a sharp vegetable peeler. First, select ripe but firm fruit. (The peaches should have very little give when gently squeezed but should have a floral aroma at room temperature.) Then, peel them as you would peel potatoes.*

1 Preheat the oven to 375°F with one rack in the middle.

2 In a small bowl, combine ¼ cup of the sugar, the cornstarch, and the cinnamon. In a medium-size bowl, pour the sugar mixture over the peaches and toss the peaches to distribute the sugar mixture evenly. Spread the peaches on the bottom of the skillet.

3 In a medium-size bowl or a food processor, combine the flour, baking powder, salt and the remaining ½ cup sugar. Stir with a fork or pulse several times to combine.

4 Add the butter and rub it into the flour, working the lumps of butter between your fingers until only very small bits of butter remain. Work quickly so that the butter stays cold. If using a food processor, add the butter and pulse 10 times.

5 Using a fork, stir in the egg and vanilla until the mixture is dampened and about the consistency of thick cake batter.

6 Drop the mixture onto the fruit about 1 tablespoon at a time, being sure to cover the fruit. The mounds should touch one another but might still leave bits of fruit exposed.

7 Place the skillet in the oven and bake until just starting to brown, about 40 minutes.

8 Remove the skillet from the oven and transfer it to a rack to cool until warm but not hot, about 30 minutes. Leftovers can be stored for 1 day at room temperature in the skillet, covered loosely with plastic wrap. Portions can be frozen in covered containers for up to 3 months.

Variations

- *Substitute 1 cup frozen blueberries for 1 cup of the peaches.*

- *Substitute an equal volume of almond meal for the flour in the topping.*

- *Peaches not in season? Substitute 6 cups frozen peaches (about 1½ pounds).*

Spiced Apple Funnel Cakes

Yes, they might be associated with carnivals and fairs, but no one's going to complain if you make them at home.

Time: 45 minutes

Yield: About 8 funnel cakes

A big drawback to deep-frying can be the amount of oil required. The greater the volume of oil, the more it costs and the longer it takes to heat and later to cool. Fortunately, not everything requires so much oil. Funnel cakes are the perfect candidate for skillet-frying. Because skillets have so little depth to them, they need relatively little oil. And the cast iron helps keep the oil at a steady temperature.

Funnel cakes have other things going for them, too: Unlike doughnuts, there's no shaping or rising. All you need is a squeeze bottle (an old ketchup bottle works fine; it should hold at least 16 ounces). This makes handling the batter infinitely easier than trying to wrangle a funnel over hot oil. Yes, this means they could be called "squeeze bottle cakes," but let's not mess with a good thing, okay? With an assist from the skillet, these are a great special treat—one that is actually quite a bit less work than you should let on.

INGREDIENTS

1 cup unbleached all-purpose flour

1 teaspoon baking powder

2 tablespoons granulated sugar

¼ teaspoon salt

Pinch of ground or freshly grated nutmeg

¾ cup milk (see Note)

1 large egg

½ cup unsweetened applesauce

2 tablespoons neutral-flavored oil (such as canola or peanut), plus more for frying

½ teaspoon vanilla extract

Confectioners' sugar, for serving

NOTE

• *Use whole milk if available.*

Spiced Apple Funnel Cakes, page 177

1 In a medium-size bowl, whisk the flour, baking powder, granulated sugar, salt, and nutmeg until combined. In a small bowl or a measuring cup, stir the milk, egg, applesauce, oil, and vanilla until combined. Whisk into the flour mixture until the batter is smooth.

2 Transfer the batter to a squeeze bottle with a 1/4-inch opening and place the bottle in the refrigerator for about 15 minutes while the oil heats.

3 Heat about 3/4 inch oil to 350°F in the skillet over medium heat. For safety's sake, do not fill the skillet with oil beyond its halfway point. When the oil is hot enough for frying, it will bubble around the handle of a wooden spoon. Line a large plate with paper towels.

4 Remove the bottle from the refrigerator and shake it vigorously so that the batter is well combined. Holding the bottle over the skillet, gently squeeze to allow the batter to flow, starting in the center of the skillet and moving quickly outward to create overlapping squiggles that form a circle about 5 inches in diameter. If the first one doesn't come out picture-perfect, don't sweat it; your technique will improve with practice. Fry the cake until golden brown on the bottom, 1 to 2 minutes. Carefully flip the cake and cook until the second side is golden brown, 1 to 2 minutes more.

5 Transfer the finished funnel cake to the paper towel-lined plate. Return the oil to 350°F before repeating Step 4 with the remaining batter. Do not allow the oil to overheat or smoke. Turn down the heat if it does.

6 Dust the finished funnel cakes with powdered sugar. Serve hot, fresh from the skillet.

TIPS

- **The batter can be prepared the night before: Add an extra 1/4 teaspoon baking powder and follow the recipe through Step 2, leaving the batter in the refrigerator overnight.**
- **Save and reuse your frying oil. Strain it through cheesecloth, a coffee filter, or a fine sieve. Store it in a sealed container in the refrigerator for up to 3 months.**

Layered Crepe Torte with Dark Chocolate and Raspberry Jam

Time: 2 hours
Cool: 2 hours
Yield: Serves 12

Make the crepes yourself in your skillet or start with store-bought crepes before layering and baking them in the skillet.

Making your own crepes is a good skill to have in your back pocket, but grabbing a package from the supermarket is a sometimes underrated skill. Packaged shelf-stable or frozen crepes are an excellent solution for this torte if you're pressed for time. Really, there's so much else going on in this dessert (including chocolate, a *lot* of chocolate) that the difference between homemade and store-bought crepes is hardly worth a second thought.

The key to making this work in the skillet is a low baking temperature and aluminum foil over the top. The ingredients, except for the egg yolks, are already cooked when they go in the oven, so there's no need to blast them with heat. Still, the heat from the oven does perform an essential function: When the elements go into the skillet, they're very much separate layers and pieces. By the time everything has finished baking, the layers have melded into one rich, beautiful torte.

INGREDIENTS

¾ cup heavy cream

8 ounces bittersweet chocolate, chopped

1 teaspoon vanilla extract

4 large egg yolks

½ cup cream cheese (half an 8-ounce package), softened

¾ cup seedless raspberry jam

½ cup confectioners' sugar, plus more for serving

Unsalted butter, for greasing the parchment paper

9 crepes, about 9 inches in diameter (page 41; see Note; or store-bought), thawed if frozen

NOTE

- *If you make the crepes on page 41, use ¼ cup batter for each crepe to yield crepes that fill the skillet.*

1 Preheat the oven to 325°F with one rack in the middle.

2 Heat the cream in the skillet over medium heat until very hot but not boiling. Carefully pour the cream into a medium-size bowl. You can also microwave the cream in a medium-size microwave-safe bowl. Stir the chocolate and vanilla into the cream. Allow to stand for 5 minutes, then whisk until the chocolate is melted and

the mixture is smooth. If the cream cools too much for the chocolate to melt, set the bowl in a sink with hot water about halfway up the side of the bowl for a few minutes, then whisk until smooth. Whisk in 2 of the egg yolks.

3 In another medium-size bowl, combine the cream cheese, jam, and confectioners' sugar. Use a whisk or a hand-held mixer on medium speed to mix until smooth. Add the remaining 2 egg yolks and whisk or beat on medium speed until combined.

4 Line the bottom of the skillet with a circle of parchment paper (see Tip), then butter the parchment and the sides of the skillet. Press a crepe onto the parchment. Cut 2 crepes in half and line the sides of the skillet with them, cut sides toward the center. The edges should slightly overlap the bottom crepe. The tops may hang over the edge of the skillet a bit.

5 Spread about ½ cup of the chocolate filling on top of the crepe, to the edge. Top with another crepe and press down with your hands to flatten it. (Flattening it keeps the filling from piling up in the center and helps the layers stay even.) Spread about ½ cup of the raspberry filling on top, to the edge, top with another crepe, and press down once again to flatten it. Repeat this process, layering with the rest of the two fillings and the remaining 4 crepes, ending with 1 crepe. Finish by folding the overhanging crepes over the top.

6 Cut a circle of parchment paper with about a 10-inch diameter (see Tip). Butter the parchment and press it on top of the stack. Cover the skillet tightly with aluminum foil. Bake for 45 minutes.

7 Remove the skillet from the oven, transfer it to a rack, remove the foil, and allow to cool for 1 hour.

8 Remove the parchment from the top and run a knife around the sides of the skillet. Place a large plate upside down over the skillet, and, keeping the plate and skillet together, invert the torte onto the plate. Lift the skillet off the torte and remove the parchment paper. Allow the torte to cool completely, about 1 hour.

9 Slice the torte and dust the slices with confectioners' sugar just before serving. Leftovers can be stored for 1 day at room temperature, covered loosely with plastic wrap. Slices can be wrapped in plastic wrap and frozen in a zip-top freezer bag for up to 3 months.

Variation

- *The list of jams that work well with chocolate is long and varied. Try mixed berry, sour cherry, apricot, or blueberry.*

TIP

- **To cut parchment paper rounds: Start with a square of parchment paper a little larger than the bottom of the skillet. Fold twice to yield a smaller square of four layers. (It will be one-quarter the size of the original.) Now make a triangle: Make the tip of the triangle the point that corresponds to the middle of the original sheet of parchment, and fold the square in half to form a triangle. Keep the tip in the same place and fold again to make an even narrower triangle. Don't worry if the edges of the triangle are ragged. Line up the tip with the center of the skillet and cut the parchment just beyond where it hits the edge of the skillet. Unfold the parchment, place it in the bottom of the skillet to check for size, and fold it to trim it, a very little bit at a time, if necessary.**

Upside Down Apricot Skillet Cake

Time: 1 hour 15 minutes
Cool: 1 hour
Yield: Serves 8

Apricots top my list of fruits that improve with cooking.

I have spent a lot of time thinking about fruit. For a while, it was paid time (I worked for an orchard). My job left me with almost unmanageable quantities of free fruit. The job ended; the fruit contemplation did not.

Peaches and apricots are related to each other—and to almonds, incidentally. Their flavors can overlap, but to my mind the texture of apricots makes them slightly better candidates for baking than for eating out of hand. Make no mistake: I have snacked on plenty of apricots, but there is no substitute for their silky texture and lightly perfumed flavor when baked.

Here, the cake itself is only lightly sweet, providing a perfect backdrop for the sweet-tart flavor of the apricots.

Coming up with this recipe meant figuring out just the right amount of fruit and batter without letting the batter run over the rim of the skillet when it cooks. That took six cakes. By cake number seven, I was just making it to make it.

Placing the apricot halves skin side down in the skillet protects the flesh of the fruit from burning. Don't worry about the rounded end of the fruit poking above the cake's surface once it's turned over; it all cooks down and flattens to perfection.

INGREDIENTS

Topping

4 tablespoons (¹/₂ stick) unsalted butter

¹/₂ cup firmly packed light brown sugar

1 pound fresh apricots (8 to 11 apricots; see Note), cut in half from top to bottom and pitted

Cake

1¹/₂ cups unbleached all-purpose flour

1¹/₂ teaspoons baking powder

¹/₂ teaspoon baking soda

¹/₂ teaspoon salt

8 tablespoons (1 stick) unsalted butter, softened

¹/₂ cup granulated sugar

2 teaspoons vanilla extract

2 large eggs

³/₄ cup buttermilk

Full-fat Greek yogurt and fresh raspberries, for serving

NOTE:

• *As a rough guide: If your apricots are about 2 inches from top to bottom, it will take 8 apricots to make 1 pound. If they are about 1¹/₂ inches from top to bottom, it will take 11 apricots to make 1 pound.*

1 Preheat the oven to 375°F with one rack in the middle.

2 Make the topping: Melt the butter in the skillet over medium-low heat until the foam subsides, about 4 minutes.

3 With the skillet over low heat, sprinkle the brown sugar evenly across the butter, then cook 3 minutes. Do not stir. Not all of the sugar will melt. Remove the skillet from the heat and arrange the apricot halves, skin side down, atop the brown sugar. They should be close together, with the edges touching but not overlapping. (Crowding the skillet could make the batter spill over the edges when the cake rises.)

4 Make the cake: In a small bowl, combine the flour, baking powder, baking soda, and salt.

5 In a large bowl, using a hand-held mixer, or in the bowl of a stand mixer fitted with the whisk, beat the butter, granulated sugar, and vanilla on medium-high speed until pale and fluffy, about 4 minutes. Add the eggs and beat on medium high until well combined, about 3 minutes, scraping down the bowl as necessary.

6 Add half of the flour mixture to the butter mixture and mix on low speed until just combined. Add half the buttermilk and mix on low until just combined. Repeat with the remaining flour and buttermilk.

7 Pour the batter evenly over the apricots and use a spatula to gently spread it.

8 Bake the cake until golden brown and a toothpick inserted in the center comes out clean, 40 to 45 minutes. Remove the skillet from the oven and transfer it to a rack to cool for 10 minutes.

9 Wearing oven mitts and taking care because the skillet is still hot, place a large plate upside down over the skillet. Keeping the plate and skillet together, invert the cake onto the plate. Lift the skillet off the cake and replace any of the fruit that may have stuck to the bottom of the skillet.

10 Cool the cake until warm or room temperature, about 1 hour. Slice and serve with a dollop of Greek yogurt and a handful of raspberries. Leftovers can be stored for 1 day at room temperature, covered loosely with plastic wrap. Slices can be wrapped in plastic wrap and frozen in a zip-top freezer bag for up to 3 months.

Variation

- *To highlight the apricot's almond family resemblance, add 1/4 teaspoon almond extract in Step 5.*

Skillet-Deep Apple Pie

This double-crusted pie takes advantage of the depth of the skillet for a hefty, unabashedly apple-y filling.

Time: 2 hours
Cool: 1 hour
Yield: Serves 8

The fact that there are so many hacks and tricks out there for pie crust should tell you that it can be persnickety. There's the vodka trick. (I know what you're thinking, but it goes in the crust.) Then there's the cream cheese trick. (Also in the crust, though that probably requires less clarification.)

Once you find a method that works, there is great incentive to stick with it. It's a scary world out there, full of people telling you they know how to make pie crust. Some of them are right. Some are not. How do you know? You try them all. Or you take the word of someone who has.

I am a strong partisan of the method devised by J. Kenji López-Alt of Serious Eats and *The Food Lab* fame and distinction. His method turns the butter and some of the flour into a paste first. Only then is the remaining flour added. It leads to a supple dough that doesn't require as much water. It works. This is the method on which I have based my recipe.

Few things are as suited for the aesthetics of the skillet as a double-crusted apple pie. Disposable pie tins and purchased pies have their place. But when it comes to presenting the best of what autumn has to offer against the deep and rough black of a well-loved skillet, it's a match made in heaven.

INGREDIENTS

Crust

2¾ cups unbleached all-purpose flour, plus more for rolling

2 tablespoons granulated sugar

½ teaspoon salt

½ pound plus 6 tablespoons (2¾ sticks) unsalted butter, cut into pats about 1 tablespoon each

7 tablespoons ice water

Filling and finishing

¼ cup firmly packed light or dark brown sugar

¼ cup plus 2 tablespoons granulated sugar

2 tablespoons cornstarch

¾ teaspoon ground cinnamon

Pinch of ground or freshly grated nutmeg

Pinch of salt

8 medium-size tart apples (about 3¼ pounds), such as Cortland, McIntosh, or Granny Smith, peeled, cored, and cut into 8 wedges each

1 tablespoon freshly squeezed lemon juice

1 tablespoon milk

1 Make the crust: In a food processor, combine 1¾ cups of the flour with the sugar and salt. Add the butter and pulse until no dry flour remains. The mixture should collect into a dough with a texture resembling children's modeling clay. The number of pulses will depend on your machine; it could take 30 pulses or it could take 50. What you're looking for is the change in texture. Break up any large clumps of dough and scrape down any stuck to the sides of the bowl. Sprinkle in the remaining 1 cup flour and pulse until the flour is just barely incorporated, about 5 pulses.

2 Transfer the dough to a large bowl. Sprinkle the water over the dough, lightly mixing with a spatula as you go. Gather the dough with the spatula, gently pressing it until large clumps hold together.

3 Divide the mixture into two equal parts, and place each on a piece of plastic wrap. Bring the edges of the plastic wrap together to gather and press the dough into a cohesive mass. Pat each piece of dough into a disk. Refrigerate for 30 minutes or freeze for 10 minutes.

4 Dust a work surface with flour. Remove one portion of the dough from the refrigerator and remove the plastic wrap. Save the plastic wrap; it can be reused in Step 6. Dust the top of the dough with flour. Use a rolling pin to press the dough into a circle about 14 inches in diameter, using light pressure, and rolling from the center out. Rotate the dough occasionally to encourage an even shape, and add flour as necessary to prevent sticking. The dough may also be returned to the refrigerator or placed in the freezer if it becomes too pliable to handle easily.

5 Place your skillet over the dough to check for size. There should be enough dough to cover the bottom and run up the sides. Transfer the dough to the skillet: Make sure the top and bottom are lightly dusted with flour so the dough won't stick to itself. Fold it in quarters, then unfold it in the skillet. Once the dough is in the skillet, press it onto the bottom and against the sides. It may hang over the edges of the skillet. That's okay; it will be trimmed later.

6 Refrigerate the skillet with the bottom crust while you follow Step 4 to roll out the second portion of dough. Once the crust is 14 inches in diameter, place it between two pieces of plastic wrap and refrigerate it while you prepare the filling. (Yes, the top crust should also be 14 inches; it doesn't need to roll up the sides of the skillet, but it will need to fit over the mounds of apples in the filling.) If it needs to be folded to fit in your refrigerator, make sure the dough is lightly coated in flour so that it doesn't stick to itself.

7 Preheat the oven to 375°F with one rack in the middle.

8 Make the filling: In a small bowl, combine the brown sugar, ¼ cup granulated sugar, the cornstarch, cinnamon, nutmeg, and salt.

9 In a large bowl, toss the apples with the lemon juice. Add the sugar mixture and toss well to distribute it evenly.

10 Remove the skillet from the refrigerator and pile the apples into the bottom crust, mounding the apples a little higher in the center.

11 Remove the top crust from the refrigerator, remove the top piece of plastic wrap, and drape the crust across the skillet. Carefully remove the remaining plastic wrap. Trim off anything hanging beyond ½ inch past the edge of the skillet. Seal the edges by rolling the bottom and top crusts together onto the rim of the skillet, then crimping them with a fork. If the fork sticks to the pastry, dip it in flour.

12 Brush the top crust with the milk, then dust it with the remaining 2 tablespoons granulated sugar. Use a sharp knife to cut three vents about 2 inches long each into the top crust to allow steam to escape.

13 Place the skillet in the oven and bake until the top crust is golden brown, about 1 hour.

14 Remove the skillet from the oven and transfer it to a rack to cool for at least 1 hour before serving the pie warm or at room temperature. Leftovers can be stored for 1 day at room temperature in the skillet, covered loosely with plastic wrap. Slices can be wrapped in plastic wrap and frozen in a zip-top freezer bag for up to 3 months.

TIPS

- **If the crust tears while rolling, it can be repaired by stealing a piece of dough from a ragged edge and adhering it to the trouble spot with a dab of ice water.**
- **Don't throw away those crust trimmings! Make them into thumbprint cookies: Preheat the oven to 350°F. Double each scrap's thickness by folding it over and pressing it together. Make a dent in the center of each scrap with your thumb. Lay the scraps in the skillet and place a dab of jam in each dent. Don't overfill with jam; it will become runny and spread out as it cooks. Bake until the cookies are golden brown, about 25 minutes.**
- **You can also turn leftover crust into savory hors d'oeuvres: Preheat the oven to 350°F. Double each scrap's thickness by folding it over and pressing it together. Lay the scraps in the skillet and sprinkle them with Gomashio (page 48). Bake until the scraps are golden brown, about 25 minutes.**

Appendix:
Developing Your Own Skillet Recipes

At this point, I hope you're looking around your kitchen and thinking, "Well . . . will it skillet?" Here are some considerations when answering the question for yourself.

Oven vs. Stovetop

Part of the skillet's strength is its versatility. It's comfortable with anything from a blast of heat from the broiler to a gentle stovetop simmer. This means that maximizing the advantages of the skillet can mean devising recipes that combine stovetop cooking with oven or broiler cooking. The Apple–Sour Cream Skillet-Size Pancake (page 29) and the Bacon-Potato Skillet Bread (page 79) are two such recipes—but it doesn't have to end there.

Cooking Times

It's appealing to combine all of the ingredients in the skillet, put it in the oven, and end up with a complete dish. (Consider the Giant Chocolate Chip Skillet Cookie, page 153.) But don't be hemmed in by that. If items require different cooking times, there are two ways to approach it. An item can be cooked and then removed from the skillet before being added back in (as in the Scallop Risotto, page 145). Or, an item can simply go in first and stay there, getting a head start on the rest of the ingredients, like the tofu in the Peanut and Tofu Skillet Stir-Fry (page 97).

Heat Characteristics

One thing to consider when adapting or developing a recipe for the skillet is its unique heat characteristics. Because it retains heat so well, you may find that items that stay in the skillet for a while after they're baked (for example, Chocolate Cake, page 165) need a slightly lower temperature because they actually continue to cook once they're out of the oven. This is less of an issue for items that are removed from the skillet and served immediately, although one aspect still bears keeping in mind: Because the cast-iron skillet retains heat so well, preheating and cooking on the same temperature, especially for long periods of time, can mean that the skillet gets very hot as the heat builds and builds. If you're unfamiliar with how a certain recipe works in a skillet, keep an eye on it and don't be afraid to turn down the heat on the stovetop once it gets going.

Volume

Remember that a skillet 10 inches in diameter with a depth of 2 inches has a volume of about 10 cups. To avoid spillovers on the stovetop, you need to max out somewhere below that number to give yourself a margin of error and make sure you're not cooking with the skillet on the brink of a spillover. If you're baking—in particular something that expands when it hits the heat, such as a cake or bread—you have to leave it room to rise. There's no magic formula to determine how much something will rise and how much room to allow it, but if you're baking such a recipe in the skillet for the first time, it pays to take out a little insurance against spills by putting a baking sheet lined with aluminum foil on the shelf below the skillet. Check on the skillet and its contents occasionally by peering through the oven door.

Conversion Tables

Please note that all conversions are approximate but close enough to be useful when converting from one system to another.

Oven Temperatures

Fahrenheit	Gas Mark	Celsius
250	½	120
275	1	140
300	2	150
325	3	160
350	4	180
375	5	190
400	6	200
425	7	220
450	8	230
475	9	240
500	10	260

NOTE: Reduce the temperature by 68°F (20°C) for fan-assisted ovens.

Approximate Equivalents

1 stick butter = 8 tbs = 4 oz = ½ cup = 115 g

1 cup presifted all-purpose flour = 4.7 oz

1 cup granulated sugar = 8 oz = 220 g

1 cup (firmly packed) brown sugar = 6 oz = 220 g to 230 g

1 cup confectioners' sugar = 4½ oz = 115 g

1 cup honey or syrup = 12 oz

1 cup grated cheese = 4 oz

1 cup dried beans = 6 oz

1 large egg = about 2 oz or about 3 tbs

1 egg yolk = about 1 tb

1 egg white = about 2 tbs

Liquid Conversions

US	Imperial	Metric
2 tbs	1 fl oz	30 ml
3 tbs	1¼ fl oz	45 ml
¼ cup	2 fl oz	60 ml
⅓ cup	2½ fl oz	75 ml
⅓ cup + 1 tb	3 fl oz	90 ml
⅓ cup + 2 tbs	3½ fl oz	100 ml
½ cup	4 fl oz	125 ml
⅔ cup	5 fl oz	150 ml
¾ cup	6 fl oz	175 ml
¾ cup + 2 tbs	7 fl oz	200 ml
1 cup	8 fl oz	250 ml
1 cup + 2 tbs	9 fl oz	275 ml
1¼ cups	10 fl oz	300 ml
1⅓ cups	11 fl oz	325 ml
1½ cups	12 fl oz	350 ml
1⅔ cups	13 fl oz	375 ml
1¾ cups	14 fl oz	400 ml
1¾ cups + 2 tbs	15 fl oz	450 ml
2 cups (1 pint)	16 fl oz	500 ml
2½ cups	20 fl oz (1 pint)	600 ml
3¾ cups	1½ pints	900 ml
4 cups	1¾ pints	1 liter

Weight Conversions

US/UK	Metric	US/UK	Metric
½ oz	15 g	7 oz	200 g
1 oz	30 g	8 oz	250 g
1½ oz	45 g	9 oz	275 g
2 oz	60 g	10 oz	300 g
2½ oz	75 g	11 oz	325 g
3 oz	90 g	12 oz	350 g
3½ oz	100 g	13 oz	375 g
4 oz	125 g	14 oz	400 g
5 oz	150 g	15 oz	450 g
6 oz	175 g	1 lb	500 g

Index

Note: Page references in *italics* indicate photographs.

French-toasted waffles, *22*, 23–24
Fruit:
    dried, sticky, cutting more easily, 133
    mixed, galette, *170*, 171–73
    see also specific fruits
Frying oil, saving and reusing, 26
Funnel cakes, spiced apple, 177–79, *178*

G

Galette, mixed fruit, *170*, 171–73
Giant cinnamon bun, 37–40, *39*
Gnocchi with goat cheese and skillet
    roasted tomatoes, 134–37, *135*
Gomashio (sesame seed seasoning mix),
    46, 48
Grilled cheese, pressed, *90*, 91–92
Grilled vegetable and Cheddar nachos,
    93–94, *95*

H

Ham:
    potpie (in a skillet), 150
    quiche, potato-crusted, 99–100, *101*
Honey, 195

I

Ingredients, 11–13
    approximate equivalents for, 195
    measuring, 11–12

Italian dishes:
    fainá, or farinata (chickpea flatbread),
        61–63, *62*
    mozzarella and mushroom calzone,
        102, 103–5
    scallop risotto, 145–47, *146*
    see also Pasta; Pizza

L

Lasagna, ricotta, spinach, and mushroom,
    118–21, *119*
Layered crepe torte with dark chocolate
    and raspberry jam, 180–83, *181*
Liquid conversions, 196

M

Mac and cheese, 106, *107*
Main courses, 89–150
    carnitas, single-skillet, 122–24, *123*
    chicken potpie (in a skillet), 148–50,
        149
    couscous with apricots and cashews,
        131–33, *132*
    deep-dish pizza, 108–11, *109*
    gnocchi with goat cheese and skillet
        roasted tomatoes, 134–37, *135*
    grilled cheese, pressed, *90*, 91–92
    grilled vegetable and Cheddar nachos,
        93–94, *95*
    mac and cheese, 106, *107*

Q

R

About the Author

Daniel Shumski is a writer and editor who has hunted ramen in Tokyo for the *Washington Post* and tracked down ice cream in Buenos Aires for the *Los Angeles Times*. Between stints at the *Chicago Sun-Times* and the *Chicago Tribune*, he worked for a midwestern heirloom apple orchard. His first book, *Will It Waffle?: 53 Irresistible and Unexpected Recipes to Make in a Waffle Iron*, won praise from the *New York Times*, *People* magazine, and *Food52*. He lives in Montreal, where his French is still a work in progress.